The ADHD Christian

Richard Lowe
The Writing King

The ADHD Christian

Table of Contents

See books by Richard Lowe at
https://masterofworlds.com

Get free publishing insights and industry updates at
https://thewritingking.substack.com

For ghostwriting and book coaching services see
https://thewritingking.com

Disclaimer

This book is for informational and encouragement purposes only and is not a substitute for professional medical, psychological, or spiritual counsel. I'm not a licensed physician, psychologist, psychiatrist, therapist, or ordained minister. The content reflects my personal experiences, research, and observations about ADHD and faith, but should not be considered professional medical or psychological advice.

Medical Disclaimer: The information in this book is not intended to diagnose, treat, cure, or prevent any medical or psychological condition. ADHD is a complex neurological condition that requires proper evaluation and treatment by qualified healthcare professionals. If you suspect you have ADHD or are experiencing symptoms that interfere with your daily functioning, please consult with a licensed physician, psychiatrist, or psychologist who specializes in ADHD assessment and treatment.

Medication decisions should always be made in consultation with qualified healthcare providers who can assess your circumstances, medical history, and treatment needs. Don't start, stop, or modify any medication regimen based on information in this book without proper medical supervision.

Mental Health Disclaimer: If you are experiencing thoughts of self-harm, suicide, or are in crisis, please seek immediate professional help by contacting:

National Suicide Prevention Lifeline: 988
Crisis Text Line: Text HOME to 741741
Your local emergency services: 911 Or go to your nearest emergency room

The strategies and perspectives shared in this book are not a replacement for professional mental health treatment. If you are struggling with depression, anxiety, trauma, or other mental health concerns, please seek appropriate professional care.

Spiritual Disclaimer: The theological perspectives and spiritual insights shared in this book reflect my personal understanding and interpretation of Scripture and Christian faith. These views may not align with all denominational teachings or theological traditions. You're encouraged to study Scripture for yourself and consult with your own spiritual advisors, pastors, or trusted Christian mentors regarding matters of faith and practice.

The integration of faith and mental health discussed in this book is not intended to replace pastoral care, spiritual direction, or professional counseling when needed.

General Disclaimer: Every person's experience with ADHD is unique. The strategies, examples, and approaches described in this book may not be suitable or effective for everyone. What works for one person may not work for another. Use your own judgment and seek appropriate professional guidance when implementing any suggestions from this book.

The author and publisher disclaim any liability for any adverse effects or consequences resulting from the use of any information, suggestions, or procedures described in this book. This book is sold with the understanding that neither the author nor the publisher is engaged in rendering professional services.

Research and Information Sources: While efforts have been made to ensure the accuracy of information presented, research on ADHD continues to evolve. You're encouraged to seek current information from reputable medical and scientific sources and to verify any claims with qualified professionals.

By reading this book, you acknowledge that you understand these limitations and agree to seek appropriate professional guidance for your circumstances and needs.

Preface

I grew up in the Church of Christ, sitting in hard wooden pews every Sunday morning, Sunday evening, and Wednesday night for the first fourteen years of my life. Looking back now, with the clarity that comes from understanding ADHD, I can see why those years were such a struggle—not just spiritually, but neurologically.

The Church of Christ tradition values order, consistency, and careful adherence to biblical patterns. Services followed predictable formats: opening prayer, congregational singing without instrumental accompaniment, communion, sermon, invitation, closing prayer. The expectation was that children would sit quietly, pay attention, and absorb the spiritual instruction being offered.

My ADHD brain had other plans.

I couldn't sit still during the long sermons. My mind wandered during prayers that seemed to stretch on forever. The a cappella singing, beautiful as it was, couldn't hold my scattered attention for four verses of "Amazing Grace." I fidgeted with the communion cups, accidentally dropped hymnals during quiet moments, and asked inappropriate questions at inappropriate times.

The rejection sensitivity that I now know accompanies ADHD made every correction feel like a personal attack on my character. When adults told me to "pay attention" or "sit still," I heard "you're not good enough." When other children seemed to naturally understand behavioral expectations that mystified me, I concluded that I was fundamentally flawed in ways that made me unfit for spiritual community.

The emphasis on getting things right—the right way to worship, the right way to interpret Scripture, the right way to live a Christian life—created constant anxiety for a brain that struggled with perfectionism and executive function. I wanted desperately to please God and the adults around me, but my neurological differences made their expectations feel impossible to meet.

By the time I was fourteen, the disconnect between my internal experience and the external expectations had become unbearable. I left the church, convinced that Christianity wasn't for people like me—people who couldn't sit still, couldn't focus consistently, and couldn't seem to get the spiritual disciplines right no matter how hard they tried.

What followed were years of spiritual searching that never quite took root. I explored various religious traditions, attended different churches sporadically, and tried to piece together a faith that would accommodate my restless, seeking, scattered brain. Nothing seemed to stick. Every spiritual community I encountered seemed designed for neurotypical minds that could engage with traditional practices in traditional ways.

I carried the shame of spiritual failure alongside the shame of academic and professional struggles. The voice in my head told the same story in every context: "You're too much. You're not enough. You don't fit anywhere, not even in God's house."

Then, a few years ago, I found myself at a Christian Church in Clearwater, listening to the Ppastor preach with a combination of intellectual depth and authentic vulnerability that my ADHD brain found compelling. He didn't promise easy answers or demand perfect adherence to spiritual formulas. He talked about God's love for broken people, about Jesus's preference for outcasts and misfits, about grace that meets us in our mess instead of demanding we clean ourselves up first.

For the first time in decades, I heard a version of Christianity that had room for people like me.

In December 2024, I was baptized. Not because I had finally gotten my act together or learned to control my ADHD symptoms, but because I finally understood that God's love isn't contingent on neurotypical behavior patterns. The same God who created my scattered, intense, creative brain also designed a path to Himself that doesn't require me to become someone else first.

What I don't say in that sentence is what the year leading up to it actually cost.

I decided I wanted to be baptized and told the church. Then I waited. The church had a schedule. They did baptisms at the beach, which meant they needed the right weather, the right tide, enough people, the right day. I understood that logistically. I did not understand it emotionally.

For an ADHD brain that had finally made a decision — a hard decision, a years-in-the-making decision — being told to wait for a schedule is not a minor inconvenience. It's a test of will that the person running the schedule doesn't know they're administering. Every week I came back, the motivation I'd built up had leaked out a little more. Every time the date shifted, I had to rebuild something that doesn't rebuild easily.

A year. I was pissed for most of it. Not at God — at the gap between what I'd decided and what the institution was able to deliver. At the bar being set at 'keep showing up, keep waiting, trust the process' when my brain was running on fumes and the process kept not resolving.

I almost didn't do it. Not because I stopped believing, but because the friction was too high and my tank was too low. That's not a spiritual failure. That's an ADHD brain that needed the moment to happen before the momentum died, and an institution that didn't know that was even a consideration.

I did it anyway. December 2024, cold beach, bad weather, exactly the conditions that had been making it hard to schedule for months. I'm glad I did. But I want you to know it wasn't effortless, and if you've been waiting for your own version of that moment and the bar keeps moving — your frustration is legitimate. The wanting is real. The waiting is hard. Both things are true.

This book grows out of that realization. It's written for the ADHD Christians who have felt like spiritual failures because their brains work differently. It's for the people who have been told that their struggles with attention, organization, and emotional regulation are character issues instead of neurological differences. It's for anyone who has wondered whether there's room in God's kingdom for minds that don't fit conventional molds.

The journey from spiritual exile back to faith community taught me that the problem was never my ADHD brain. The problem was a limited understanding of how God designed different kinds of minds to serve different purposes in His kingdom. My ADHD traits aren't obstacles to overcome in my spiritual life—they're tools to understand and steward for the unique calling God has placed on my life.

If you've ever felt like Christianity wasn't designed for people like you, I hope this book will help you discover that you're not the problem. Your neurodivergent brain isn't a design flaw or a spiritual liability. It's a feature, not a bug, in God's diverse kingdom where every kind of mind has a place and a purpose.

The boy who couldn't sit still in church grew up to write this book. Make of that what you will.

Your faith walk won't look like anyone else's. That's the point. This book is an invitation to stop performing someone else's version of faith and start living your own.

Introduction

If you've picked up this book, chances are you've felt the tension of trying to live faithfully as a Christian while your ADHD brain refuses to cooperate. You've probably struggled to maintain consistent prayer and Bible reading routines. You've likely felt overwhelmed by the social demands of church life or frustrated when your mind wanders during sermons. You might have wondered if God made a mistake when He designed your scattered, hyperactive, or laser-focused mind.

You are not alone, and you are not broken.

Traditional approaches to Christian living rarely account for neurodivergent minds. Well-meaning pastors and Christian authors offer advice about daily devotions, organized spiritual disciplines, and consistent church involvement without acknowledging that these practices might need to look completely different for someone with ADHD, autism, or related traits. The result? Many sincere believers feel like spiritual failures when conventional methods don't work for their unique brains.

Your ADHD brain isn't an obstacle to overcome in your faith walk. It's part of how God designed you to know and serve Him. Your hyperfocus can become a spiritual superpower when directed toward Scripture or ministry. Your creativity and unconventional thinking can bring fresh perspectives to ancient theological questions. Your emotional intensity can deepen your empathy and compassion for others. Even your struggles with traditional spiritual disciplines can lead you to discover more authentic and sustainable ways to connect with God.

Scripture shows us God using people whose minds worked differently. David, who wrote many of the Psalms, displayed the emotional intensity and creative passion we recognize in ADHD. The apostle Paul's relentless energy and ability to shift between detailed theological arguments and passionate personal appeals suggests a mind that operated outside conventional patterns. Jesus withdrew from crowds when overstimulated and taught in ways that engaged different learning styles and attention spans.

This book sees ADHD and related neurodivergent traits through a biblical lens that views diversity of mind as part of God's creative design. Just as the body of Christ needs different gifts and abilities to function well, the church needs different types of minds and personalities. Your neurodivergent brain isn't a design flaw. It's part of how God intends to accomplish His purposes in the world.

Instead of forcing your square-peg brain into round-hole spiritual practices, this guide will help you discover ADHD-friendly approaches to prayer, Bible study, community involvement, and Christian living. You'll learn practical strategies that work with your brain instead of against it. You'll discover how your unique wiring can be a strength in your spiritual path and ministry to others.

The pages ahead address the real challenges you face: maintaining focus during prayer, managing emotional dysregulation in relationships, dealing with rejection sensitivity in church contexts, and finding sustainable rhythms for spiritual growth. But they'll also help you recognize and celebrate the gifts that come with your neurodivergent mind: creativity, empathy, innovation, crisis management skills, and the ability to see connections others miss.

Whether you're newly diagnosed with ADHD, have suspected it for years, or are supporting someone who is neurodivergent, this book meets you where you are. Each chapter includes Scripture-based foundations, practical strategies, and real-world applications that acknowledge both the struggles and strengths of the ADHD Christian experience.

Your faith walk doesn't have to look like everyone else's. God has given you a unique brain for a unique purpose. Stop apologizing for how He made you and start discovering how He wants to use you.

Part I: Foundation - Your Neurodivergent Identity in Christ

Fearfully and Wonderfully Made

"For you created my inmost being; you knit me together in my mother's womb. I praise you because I am fearfully and wonderfully made; your works are wonderful, I know that full well." (Psalm 139:13-14, NIV)

The first time someone suggested I might have ADHD, my initial reaction was denial mixed with relief. Denial because I'd spent decades believing I was just lazy, undisciplined, and spiritually immature. Relief because suddenly the scattered pieces of my life began forming a recognizable picture. The constant mental chatter during prayer wasn't a sign of weak faith. The inability to sit still during long sermons wasn't spiritual rebellion. The hyperfocus sessions that made me lose track of time weren't character flaws. My brain simply worked differently.

But then came the harder question: If God knit me together in my mother's womb, why did He include ADHD in the design? Was this part of His perfect plan, or evidence that sin had corrupted His original blueprint? The struggle to reconcile my faith with my neurodivergent that reality sent me searching in ways that challenged everything I thought I knew about God's design and my place in it.

David's words in Psalm 139 provide the theological foundation we need. When he declared himself "fearfully and wonderfully made," he wasn't speaking as someone who had it all together. This was the same David who committed adultery, orchestrated murder, struggled with depression, and wrote emotionally intense psalms that swing from despair to exultant praise within a few verses. His mind displayed traits we recognize today:

emotional intensity, creative passion, and the kind of dramatic shifts that resonate with many neurodivergent people.

David understood something profound about God's design. The Hebrew word for "fearfully" (yare) doesn't mean scary or frightening. It means with reverence, with awe-inspiring complexity. You were made with intricate, awe-inspiring complexity. The word "wonderfully" (pala) refers to something extraordinary, set apart, distinguished from the ordinary. Your ADHD brain isn't a manufacturing defect. It's an extraordinary variation in God's creative design.

> ★ **Pro Tip:** When shame spirals hit, read Psalm 139:14 out loud and replace "I" with your name. "Sarah is fearfully and wonderfully made." Say it until your nervous system starts to believe it.

Consider how this challenges our modern understanding of normal. We live in a culture that prizes conformity, consistency, and predictable behavior. The education system rewards students who can sit still, focus on demand, and process information in linear ways. The workplace values employees who thrive in structured environments, meet deadlines naturally, and maintain steady emotional regulation. The church often promotes spiritual practices that require sustained attention, quiet contemplation, and systematic approaches to growth.

God's kingdom operates on different principles. Throughout Scripture, He consistently chooses people who don't fit the conventional mold. Moses had a speech impediment. Gideon struggled with anxiety and self-doubt. Peter was impulsive and emotionally volatile. Paul was intense and single-minded to the point of obsession, with patterns of thinking and behavior that would strike many as unconventional. These weren't obstacles God had to work around. They were features He intentionally included in His plan.

★ **Pro Tip:** Create a "design features" list of your ADHD traits and write next to each one how God might use that trait for good. Your scattered attention might help you notice things others miss. Your emotional intensity might help you connect with hurting people.

Your ADHD brain comes with a unique combination of challenges and gifts. The same neurological differences that make sustained attention difficult also fuel creativity, innovation, and the ability to make connections others miss. The emotional intensity that sometimes feels overwhelming also enables deep empathy and passionate advocacy for justice. The impulsivity that gets you into trouble can also drive you to take risks others wouldn't consider, leading to breakthrough moments in ministry and relationships.

The hyperfocus that makes you lose track of time when you're engaged with something meaningful is a powerful tool for studying Scripture, solving problems, and diving deep into areas where God has called you to serve. Your need for novelty and stimulation can help you connect with people and situations that bore more conventional personalities. Your ability to think outside established patterns can bring fresh insights to ancient truths.

Jeremiah 1:5 tells us that before God formed us in the womb, He knew us. This wasn't casual acquaintance but intimate, detailed knowledge. He knew exactly how your brain would be wired. He knew you would struggle with attention regulation, emotional intensity, and executive function challenges. He also knew you would bring unique perspectives, creative solutions, and passionate engagement to His kingdom work. Both the struggles and the gifts were part of His intentional design.

This doesn't mean ADHD is easy or that we should romanticize its challenges. The difficulties are real. The frustration of forgetting important commitments, the shame of emotional outbursts, the exhaustion of constant mental chatter, the pain of rejection sensitivity are all genuine struggles that require compassion, understanding, and practical strategies. These challenges don't negate your value or disqualify you from God's purposes.

> ⚠ **Caution:** Don't use God's intentional design as an excuse to avoid growth or responsibility. Being fearfully and wonderfully made includes the responsibility to steward your gifts and manage your challenges wisely.

Paul understood this tension when he wrote about his own "thorn in the flesh" in 2 Corinthians 12. Three times he pleaded with God to remove whatever was causing him difficulty. God's response wasn't healing but something better: "My grace is sufficient for you, for my power is made perfect in weakness." Paul discovered that his limitations became the very places where God's strength was most evident.

Your ADHD brain creates space for God's grace to operate in ways that might not be necessary if everything came easily. When you struggle to maintain spiritual disciplines, you learn to depend on God's mercy instead of your own performance. When traditional approaches don't work, you're forced to be creative and discover new ways to connect with Him. When you experience rejection or misunderstanding, you develop compassion for others who feel marginalized.

The theology of neurodiversity recognizes that cognitive differences serve important purposes in God's design for humanity. Just as physical diversity enables different types of work and service, neurological diversity brings different types of thinking, problem-solving, and relating to the body of Christ. Your ADHD brain isn't a consolation prize or a cross to bear. It's a tool God has given you for His kingdom.

This perspective requires rejecting the shame that often accompanies an ADHD diagnosis. Shame tells us we're fundamentally flawed, that we need to hide our true selves to be acceptable. God's view is different. When He looks at you, He sees someone fearfully and wonderfully made, someone whose unique wiring serves important purposes in His grand design.

Your ADHD brain isn't something to overcome or apologize for. It's something to understand, steward well, and use for His glory.

I figured this out young, though I didn't have language for it then. By the time I was eight, the things that made the most sense to me weren't people. Books didn't yell at me. Model kits didn't hit me. Rocks didn't change the rules without warning. These things were reliable in ways that the humans around me simply weren't. So I built my world around them — collections, projects, systems — and inside that world I felt capable in a way I never felt anywhere else.

What looked like a kid retreating into his own head was actually a kid discovering what his brain was built for. The damage was becoming the skillset, one carefully constructed system at a time. I didn't know it then, but God was already using the wiring He'd given me, even when the circumstances around me were anything but His intention.

Your ADHD brain has probably done the same thing. The coping mechanisms you developed, the workarounds, the parallel worlds you built inside your head during boring meetings or endless church services — those weren't failures of attention. They were your brain doing exactly what it was designed to do with the material it was given.

This truth changes how you approach your faith walk. You can explore ADHD-friendly approaches that work with your brain instead of against it. You can celebrate the unique perspectives and abilities your differences bring. You can share your struggles openly, knowing they're part of how God designed you to relate to Him and serve others.

> **✕ Danger Zone:** Avoid churches or people who insist your ADHD symptoms are spiritual issues that prayer alone should fix. This theology is both medically ignorant and spiritually harmful.

The path forward isn't about fixing what's wrong with you. It's about discovering how God wants to use what's right with you. Your scattered attention can become multi-faceted awareness. Your emotional intensity can become passionate worship. Your need for stimulation can become adventurous faith. Your creative thinking can become innovative ministry. The very traits that make you feel different are the ones God intends to use for His purposes.

You are fearfully and wonderfully made, ADHD brain and all. The God who knit you together in your mother's womb included every aspect of your neurological wiring for reasons that may not always be clear but are always purposeful. Your path as an ADHD Christian isn't about becoming someone else. It's about becoming more fully yourself as God designed you to be.

> ✖ **Danger Zone:** Never let anyone convince you that taking medication or seeking therapy means you don't trust God enough. God works through medical professionals just as much as through miraculous healing.

Understanding Your ADHD Brain

Your brain is not broken. It's wired differently.

Knowing how your ADHD brain works isn't about making excuses or wallowing in self-pity. It's about recognizing the unique operating system God gave you so you can work with it instead of constantly fighting against it. When you understand why your brain does what it does, you stop interpreting every challenge as a moral failure and start seeing opportunities for creative solutions.

The ADHD brain operates like a race car with bicycle brakes. You've got this powerful engine capable of extraordinary performance, but the stopping and steering mechanisms weren't designed to handle that kind of horsepower. This creates the paradox that defines ADHD: you can hyperfocus for hours on something that captivates you but can't seem to focus for five minutes on something boring but important.

Neurologically, ADHD involves differences in how your brain produces and processes dopamine and norepinephrine, the neurotransmitters responsible for attention, motivation, and executive function. Your brain is constantly seeking stimulation to reach optimal functioning levels. When it doesn't find enough stimulation in the environment, it creates its own through daydreaming, fidgeting, or mental wandering. When it finds something truly engaging, it can lock onto it with laser focus.

Here's what hyperfocus actually looks like from the inside: I once started painting a model after breakfast and looked up to find it was dinnertime. Not because I'd lost track of time in some vague sense — I genuinely had no awareness that time was passing. Eight hours felt like twenty minutes. The model wasn't even anything important. It was a plastic replica of a World War II destroyer. But my brain had decided it mattered, and once that switch flipped, nothing else existed.

Meanwhile, five minutes of math homework felt longer than five hours of that model building. The disconnect was total. It wasn't about intelligence or effort. It was about whether my brain had decided to engage. When it did, it went all the way. When it didn't, no amount of willpower made any difference.

This is what Paul might have recognized in himself — that singular, consuming intensity that let him write half the New Testament and also drove him across the known world chasing a calling most people thought was insane. The same wiring that made him hard to live with made him impossible to stop.

This isn't laziness or lack of discipline. It's how your brain is designed to function. The same wiring that makes it hard to pay attention to a boring sermon gives you the ability to notice details others miss. The emotional sensitivity that makes criticism feel devastating also enables you to connect deeply with others' pain and joy. The impulsivity that gets you in trouble can also lead to spontaneous acts of generosity and breakthrough moments of insight.

Paul's description of the body of Christ in Romans 12 provides a perfect framework for understanding neurodiversity. Just as hands and feet serve different functions but are equally valuable parts of the body, different types of brains serve different functions in God's kingdom. Your ADHD brain isn't a defective version of a "normal" brain. It's a different type of brain with its own strengths and purposes.

Think about how this plays out in real life. Your neurotypical friend might excel at systematic Bible study, reading through Scripture methodically and taking careful notes. You might struggle with that approach but discover profound truths while listening to worship music or taking a prayer walk. Neither approach is superior. They're just different ways of engaging with God that match different brain types.

Your emotional intensity can feel like a curse when you're overwhelmed by criticism or rejection, but it becomes a superpower when channeled toward worship, compassion, or advocacy for justice. David's psalms resonate with ADHD brains precisely because they capture that emotional intensity. One moment he's crying out in despair, the next he's praising God with exuberant joy. That's not emotional instability. That's authentic engagement with life and faith.

The executive function challenges that come with ADHD affect planning, organization, time management, and emotional regulation. These are the "bicycle brakes" trying to control the race car engine. You might have brilliant ideas but struggle to implement them systematically. You might care deeply about people but forget to follow through on commitments. You might feel emotions intensely but have trouble regulating them appropriately.

Seeing these challenges clearly removes the moral judgment from your struggles. When you forget an important appointment, it's not because you don't care. It's because your brain has difficulty with working memory and time awareness. When you interrupt people in conversation, it's not because you're rude. It's because your brain processes thoughts faster than your impulse control can filter them. When you procrastinate on important tasks, it's not because you're lazy. It's because your brain needs higher levels of stimulation to engage with unstimulating activities.

> ★ **Pro Tip:** Schedule demanding tasks during your natural peak attention times instead of forcing yourself to work when your brain is offline. Most ADHD brains have 2-3 hours of optimal focus per day. Guard those hours fiercely.

Rejection Sensitive Dysphoria (RSD) deserves special attention because it profoundly affects how ADHD brains experience relationships and criticism. RSD isn't just being sensitive to rejection. It's an intense emotional reaction to perceived criticism, rejection, or failure that feels like physical pain. For many ADHD Christians, RSD makes church environments challenging because any correction, suggestion, or even well-meaning advice can trigger overwhelming shame and emotional dysregulation.

This hypersensitivity to rejection often develops as a protective response to years of criticism and misunderstanding. If you've spent your childhood being told to sit still, pay attention, and try harder, your brain develops early warning systems to detect any hint of disapproval. The same neural pathways that make you emotionally intense also make you acutely aware of social dynamics and potential rejection.

ADHD doesn't stay in your head. It lives in your body.

By the time I was ten, I was making regular late-night trips to the emergency room with stomach pain so severe it doubled me over. Every test came back normal. "Probably just stress," the doctor would say, in the dismissive tone adults use when they can't find anything to fix. The pain was real. The cause just wasn't showing up on any X-ray.

The migraines were worse. Pain that started behind one eye and spread like wildfire until sound was unbearable and light felt like a physical assault. I lived on aspirin. The pharmacist started giving me worried looks when I showed up with my allowance money for the third time in a week.

Nobody connected any of this to how my brain was processing the world around me. Nobody asked what a child's nervous system does when it's in a constant state of hypervigilance, scanning for threats, unable to regulate, never fully at rest. The answer, it turns out, is that it breaks down. Not because something is wrong with you spiritually or morally. Because your nervous system has limits, and ADHD pushes hard against all of them.

If your body carries stress in ways that seem disproportionate to the situation, this is why. The church's answer is usually "give it to God." That's true and incomplete. Your nervous system also needs practical relief, physical regulation, and sometimes professional support. God works through all three.

But here's what's remarkable: the same sensitivity that makes criticism feel devastating also gives you incredible empathy and emotional intelligence. You can read the room, sense when someone is struggling, and respond with compassion because your brain is constantly monitoring emotional cues. This makes you naturally gifted at pastoral care, counseling, and ministry to hurting people.

The hyperfocus aspect of ADHD is perhaps the most misunderstood. People see you unable to focus on homework or household chores and assume you have an attention deficit. When something captures your interest, you can focus with an intensity that neurotypical brains can't match. You lose track of time, forget to eat, and become completely absorbed in the activity. This isn't selective attention or laziness. It's a different type of attention system.

> ★ **Pro Tip:** Learn to recognize your hyperfocus triggers and redirect them strategically. If you tend to hyperfocus on organizing when stressed, use that pattern to tackle important projects during high-stress seasons.

Hyperfocus can become a spiritual discipline when directed toward prayer, Scripture study, or ministry activities. Some of the most profound spiritual insights come during these states of intense engagement. The key is learning to recognize what triggers hyperfocus for you and structuring your spiritual life to take advantage of these natural patterns.

Your brain also craves novelty and stimulation, which can make traditional spiritual disciplines feel stale and boring. This same need for variety can lead you to explore different prayer styles, worship expressions, and ministry opportunities. You might discover Celtic spirituality, contemplative practices, or social justice work that ignites your passion in ways that conventional approaches never could.

★ **Pro Tip:** Keep a "win journal" to track when your ADHD traits help you succeed. Write down examples: "My hyperfocus helped me solve that problem everyone else was stuck on" or "My pattern recognition spotted the issue in the budget." Your brain needs evidence of its strengths.

The ADHD brain's ability to make unusual connections between disparate ideas is a tremendous gift for understanding Scripture and theology. While others might study the Bible systematically, you might notice thematic connections across different books, see modern applications for ancient principles, or understand metaphors and parables in creative ways. Your non-linear thinking can bring fresh perspectives to familiar passages.

Working memory challenges affect how you process and retain information, which can make traditional teaching methods less effective. You might struggle to follow long sermons or complex theological arguments but excel at experiential learning, discussion-based Bible studies, or hands-on ministry activities. Understanding this helps you choose learning environments that match your brain's strengths.

⚠ **Caution:** Don't assume every struggle is ADHD-related. Some things are just hard for everyone, and attributing everything to ADHD can prevent you from developing necessary skills or seeking appropriate help.

Time blindness is another common ADHD trait that affects spiritual life. You might intend to spend 15 minutes in prayer and suddenly realize two hours have passed, or you might think you've been praying for a long time when it's only been three minutes. This makes traditional time-based spiritual disciplines challenging but opens up opportunities for more flexible, natural rhythms of spiritual engagement.

The key to working with your ADHD brain is accepting its design instead of fighting it. This doesn't mean giving up on growth or making excuses for harmful behavior. It means understanding your neurological patterns and finding ways to channel them constructively. When you stop trying to force your brain into neurotypical patterns and start honoring its unique wiring, you discover that many of the traits you've seen as weaknesses are strengths waiting to be developed.

Your ADHD brain is part of God's diverse design for His body. The challenges are real and require practical strategies, but they don't disqualify you from spiritual growth or kingdom service. They simply mean your path will look different from others, and that's exactly what God intended. In a world that often values conformity and predictability, your neurodivergent brain brings creativity, passion, and fresh perspectives that the church desperately needs.

> ⚠ **Caution:** Avoid using your ADHD diagnosis as a complete identity. You are a complex person who happens to have ADHD, not an ADHD person who happens to have other traits.

Knowing your brain is the first step toward embracing the unique way God has called you to know and serve Him. The same neural differences that create challenges in some areas also create extraordinary abilities in others. Learning to recognize, understand, and steward these differences is part of becoming the person God designed you to be.

Building Sustainable Spiritual Disciplines

"Blessed is the one who does not walk in step with the wicked or stand in the way that sinners take or sit in the company of mockers, but whose delight is in the law of the Lord, and who meditates on his law day and night." (Psalm 1:2-3, NIV)

"Come to me, all you who are weary and burdened, and I will give you rest. Take my yoke upon you and learn from me, for I am gentle and humble in heart, and you will find rest for your souls. For my yoke is easy and my burden light." (Matthew 11:28-30, NIV)

The guilt hits at 11:47 PM as you're scrolling through your phone, realizing you forgot to do your "quiet time" again. You promise yourself you'll wake up early tomorrow and spend an hour reading Scripture and praying. You set three alarms. You wake up at 6 AM with good intentions, but your brain immediately starts racing with thoughts about the day ahead. You sit down with your Bible, read two verses, and your mind wanders to that conversation you had yesterday, then to what you need to buy at the grocery store, then to whether you remembered to pay that bill.

After ten minutes of fighting your scattered attention, you give up and tell yourself you're a spiritual failure. Sound familiar?

I spent years doing exactly what my father modeled: sitting motionless in those wooden pews every Sunday, unfocusing my eyes, letting my mind race through books I'd read, projects I wanted to build, anything that could keep me functional while my body performed the required stillness. The same hyperfocus that let me read for eight hours straight became a survival tool for enduring religious theater.

I got very good at looking like I was paying attention. I was not paying attention. I was somewhere else entirely — somewhere my brain had chosen because the alternative was a kind of slow suffocation that ten-year-olds don't have words for. The grown-ups around me would have called this disrespectful. What it actually was, I now understand, was my nervous system doing the only thing it could do to survive an environment it wasn't built for.

If you've spent years performing spiritual disciplines without actually connecting to anything, you're not alone and you're not a failure. You may just be using the wrong method for your brain type. The goal was never the performance. It was always the connection. For ADHD brains, those two things are often in direct conflict.

⚠ **Caution:** Don't abandon spiritual disciplines entirely during chaotic seasons. Scale down instead of stopping completely. Even 30 seconds of prayer maintains the connection and prevents the shame spiral of starting over from zero.

Traditional spiritual disciplines were designed by and for neurotypical brains. The assumption is that with enough willpower and dedication, anyone can maintain consistent daily routines of prayer, Bible reading, and meditation. Your ADHD brain operates differently. It needs movement, variety, stimulation, and flexibility. Trying to force it into rigid spiritual routines is like trying to run racing fuel through a lawn mower engine. It's not going to work, and you'll burn out the motor.

Jesus said His yoke is easy and His burden is light. If your approach to spiritual disciplines feels heavy, burdensome, and impossible to maintain, you're probably using the wrong yoke. The goal isn't to develop superhuman discipline or to prove your spiritual worth through consistent performance. The goal is to connect with God in ways that match how He designed your brain to function.

Let's start with prayer, the spiritual discipline that trips up more ADHD Christians than any other. The traditional model involves sitting quietly, closing your eyes, and focusing your mind on God for extended periods. For your brain, this is torture. Within thirty seconds, you're thinking about lunch, analyzing a conversation from three days ago, or planning your weekend. You try to refocus, but the mental chatter continues. Eventually, you give up and assume you're bad at prayer.

You're not bad at prayer. You're just using the wrong method for your brain type. Prayer is simply communication with God, and communication can happen in countless ways. Your ADHD brain might connect with God more effectively through walking prayers, where the physical movement helps regulate your attention. Or through praying with your eyes open while looking at nature. Or through writing prayers in a journal where your thoughts can flow freely without getting lost.

Some ADHD Christians discover that fidget tools enhance their prayer life instead of distracting from it. A stress ball, prayer beads, or even a small toy can occupy the restless part of your brain while allowing the focused part to engage with God. This isn't disrespectful or childish. It's working with your neurological design.

Visual aids can transform prayer for the ADHD brain. Instead of trying to maintain abstract focus, you might pray while looking at pictures, icons, or even while doodling. Your brain processes visual information differently, and engaging that pathway can deepen your prayer experience instead of diminishing it.

★ **Pro Tip:** Use "habit stacking" by attaching spiritual disciplines to existing routines. Pray while your coffee brews, read scripture during lunch breaks, or practice gratitude while brushing your teeth. Your brain loves piggybacking new habits onto established ones.

Fixed prayer schedules fail ADHD brains for obvious reasons — time blindness, variable attention, the all-or-nothing spiral when you miss a day. Instead: two minutes when you wake up, five at lunch, three before bed. Or set random alarms for thirty-second prayer breaks throughout the day. Micro-prayers that actually happen beat hour-long sessions you keep rescheduling.

Bible study has the same problem. Traditional approaches involve systematic reading plans, detailed notes, and linear progression through books. Your brain probably hates all of that. It might engage better with thematic studies that jump between passages, audio Bibles you can absorb while walking, or apps that include video and maps. Whatever keeps you in the text instead of staring at it.

The hyperfocus aspect of your brain can be a tremendous asset for Bible study when you find passages or topics that capture your interest. Instead of fighting this natural tendency, lean into it. When something in Scripture grabs your attention, dive deep. Spend hours exploring cross-references, commentaries, and related passages. These intensive study sessions often yield more spiritual growth than months of forced daily readings.

Consider alternative Bible study methods that match your learning style. Instead of always reading silently, try reading aloud, engaging both visual and auditory processing. Copy verses by hand, helping with retention and focus. Use different Bible translations to see familiar passages in new ways. Create mind maps or visual summaries of biblical concepts. These approaches might seem unconventional, but they work with your brain instead of against it.

> **⚠ Caution:** Avoid spiritual disciplines that consistently trigger your ADHD challenges without providing spiritual benefit. If traditional lectio divina never works for you, try audio Bible apps or walking prayer instead. *Place after:*

Meditation, perhaps the most challenging traditional discipline for ADHD brains, needs complete redefinition. The goal of Christian meditation isn't to empty your mind but to focus it on God's truth. For your brain, this might happen more effectively through active meditation: repeating Scripture verses while walking, focusing on God's attributes while doing simple tasks, or practicing breath prayers that give your mind something concrete to focus on.

Movement-based meditation can be effective. Walking labyrinths, hiking while focusing on God's creation, or even pacing while reciting Scripture can help your brain settle into a meditative state. The key is finding the right balance of physical activity to quiet mental restlessness without creating too much distraction.

Sustainable spiritual routines require understanding your natural rhythms and energy patterns. Your brain might be most focused in the morning, late at night, or after physical exercise. Instead of forcing yourself into arbitrary schedules, pay attention to when you naturally feel most alert and spiritually open. Schedule your primary spiritual activities during these peak times.

> **★ Pro Tip:** Create multiple short spiritual practices instead of one long session. Five 3-minute prayer breaks throughout the day often work better for ADHD brains than one 15-minute block.

Habit stacking can be more effective than creating standalone spiritual disciplines. Attach prayer to activities you already do consistently: pray while brewing your morning coffee, listen to worship music during your commute, or reflect on Scripture verses while brushing your teeth. This uses existing routines instead of requiring entirely new ones.

The all-or-nothing thinking that often accompanies ADHD can sabotage spiritual growth. You miss one day of Bible reading and assume you've failed completely. You have a distracted prayer time and conclude you're spiritually immature. This perfectionist mindset is antithetical to grace and hinders spiritual development.

Embrace inconsistent consistency. Your spiritual life might look like three days of intense Scripture study followed by a week of quick prayer texts to God throughout the day. That's not spiritual failure. That's working with your brain's natural rhythms. God cares more about the overall trajectory of your heart toward Him than about perfect daily performance.

Seasonal approaches can work better than rigid year-round routines. Your brain might engage deeply with Advent practices in December, intensive Scripture memorization in summer, or contemplative prayer during Lent. Allow your spiritual practices to ebb and flow with your natural cycles of interest and energy.

Community can provide the external structure that your brain struggles to create internally. Joining a small group Bible study gives you built-in accountability and social motivation. Finding a prayer partner creates external commitment that helps overcome executive function challenges. Participating in corporate worship provides structure and community energy that individual disciplines might lack.

Technology can be your friend in developing spiritual disciplines. Bible apps with built-in reminders, prayer apps that guide your focus, worship playlists that create atmosphere, and social features that connect you with other believers can all support your spiritual growth. Don't let spiritual pride keep you from using tools that help your brain engage with God.

The key to building sustainable spiritual disciplines is experimentation without judgment. Try different approaches for reasonable periods. If something doesn't work, it's not because you're spiritually deficient. It's because that method doesn't match your brain's design. Keep experimenting until you find practices that feel life-giving instead of burdensome.

Remember that spiritual disciplines are means, not ends. The goal isn't perfect execution of religious practices. The goal is deepening your relationship with God and growing in Christlikeness. If a discipline isn't serving that purpose, it's okay to modify it or try something different.

> ✘ **Danger Zone:** Avoid guilt-based motivation for spiritual practices. "I should pray more" creates shame cycles that destroy long-term growth. Instead, focus on "I get to connect with God" or "This practice helps me feel more grounded."

Your ADHD brain might never master traditional spiritual disciplines, and that's perfectly fine. God didn't design spiritual growth to happen only through conventional methods. He designed it to happen through authentic relationship with Him, and that relationship can flourish through whatever practices genuinely connect your unique brain with His heart.

The spiritual disciplines that transform your life will probably look different from what you see in books or what works for your neurotypical friends. That's not a bug in the system. That's a feature. God's kingdom is big enough for all kinds of minds and all kinds of spiritual practices. Your job isn't to conform to someone else's template. It's to discover the unique ways God has designed you to know and love Him.

Part II: Navigating Daily Life - ADHD and Christian Living

Focus and Attention in a Distracted World

"Finally, brothers and sisters, whatever is true, whatever is noble, whatever is right, whatever is pure, whatever is lovely, whatever is admirable—if anything is excellent or praiseworthy—think about such things." (Philippians 4:8, NIV)

"Martha, Martha," the Lord answered, "you are worried and upset about many things, but few things are needed—or indeed only one. Mary has chosen what is better, and it will not be taken away from her." (Luke 10:41-42, NIV)

You sit down to read your Bible with the best of intentions. You open to where you left off yesterday and start reading. Three verses in, your mind wanders to the conversation you had with your coworker about the project deadline. You catch yourself, refocus on Scripture, and read another verse. Suddenly you're thinking about whether you remembered to pay that bill. You snap back to the Bible, read the same verse twice because you weren't really paying attention the first time, and then notice a notification pop up on your phone.

> ★ **Pro Tip:** Use the "notification fast" during spiritual time. Turn off all non-essential alerts for designated periods. Your phone doesn't need to ping every time someone likes your social media post or sends a non-urgent email.

Twenty minutes later, you've read maybe five verses, checked three social media apps, responded to two text messages, and added four items to your mental to-do list. You close your Bible feeling frustrated and spiritually defeated, wondering why you can't even focus on God's Word for ten uninterrupted minutes.

Welcome to attention in the 21st century with an ADHD brain. You're trying to focus in a world designed to scatter your attention, using a brain that already struggles with focus, while feeling guilty that your spiritual disciplines don't look like those of someone living in a monastery in 1200 AD.

The modern world has become an ADHD simulator for everyone. Constant notifications, infinite scrolling, dopamine-driven app design, and information overload create an environment that fragments attention and rewards distraction. For neurotypical brains, this is challenging but manageable. For ADHD brains, it's like trying to concentrate while someone shoots off fireworks next to your head.

★ **Pro Tip:** Practice the "sacred pause" technique. When distracting thoughts arise during prayer or Bible study, take three deep breaths and gently return attention to your spiritual practice without judging yourself for getting distracted.

Paul's instruction in Philippians 4:8 to think about things that are true, noble, right, pure, lovely, and admirable wasn't written in a world of smartphones and social media. He was writing to people whose biggest distractions might have been noise from the marketplace or thoughts about dinner. Applying this verse to modern life requires understanding both the timeless principle and the unique challenges of our current context.

Your attention operates differently from neurotypical brains. You don't have an attention deficit. You have attention dysregulation. Sometimes you can't focus on anything. Other times you hyperfocus so intensely that you forget to eat, drink, or acknowledge other human beings. Sometimes your attention bounces rapidly between multiple things. Other times it gets completely hijacked by something irrelevant to your goals.

This isn't a character flaw or spiritual immaturity. It's how your brain processes information and regulates attention. The same neural differences that make it hard to focus on boring but important tasks also give you the ability to notice details others miss, make creative connections between disparate ideas, and maintain intense focus when something truly engages you.

Stop fighting your attention patterns. Work with them instead. Traditional focus advice assumes you have a neurotypical attention system that responds predictably to willpower and environmental controls. Your attention is more like weather than a light switch. You can prepare for it, work with it, and create conditions that support it, but you can't simply decide to focus and have it happen.

I learned about sensory overload before I had a name for it. I was maybe four years old, in a paint store with my father. The automatic doors slid open and the place hit me like a wall — color samples covering every surface, fluorescent lights buzzing overhead, turpentine sharp in the air, voices ricocheting off hard walls, paint cans clattering as employees restocked. My navigation system short-circuited completely. I drifted into the shelving maze and grabbed what I thought were my father's pants. They weren't.

The stranger looked down at me with kind eyes and said, "Excuse me, son, but you're not my kid."

I screamed.

What my parents interpreted as embarrassing behavior was something simpler and more neurological: my brain had taken in more sensory information than it could process, lost its spatial bearings, and panicked. Not a character flaw. Not defiance. A system that had hit its limit.

Modern life is that paint store, running on an infinite loop. The environment you're trying to focus in was not designed for your brain. Every notification, every competing demand, every open-plan office or loud sanctuary is another source of input hitting a system that's already working overtime just to filter out the noise. Knowing this doesn't fix it. But it stops you from interpreting every attention failure as a spiritual or moral one.

> ⚠ **Caution:** Don't attempt to eliminate all stimulation during spiritual practices. Your ADHD brain might need background music, fidget tools, or movement to maintain attention. Experiment to find your optimal stimulation level.

Knowing your personal attention patterns is the first step toward managing them. Some ADHD brains focus better with background noise, others need complete silence. Some focus better in the morning, others late at night. Some need movement to think clearly, others need to be still. Some focus better when slightly understimulated, others when slightly overstimulated. Pay attention to when and where you naturally focus best, then structure your important activities around those patterns.

Single-tasking is a spiritual discipline for ADHD brains. The myth of multitasking is particularly damaging for neurodivergent minds — it promises efficiency and delivers scattered attention and extra guilt. Your brain performs better when focused on one thing at a time, even though it naturally wants to jump between multiple things.

> ★ **Pro Tip:** Create "attention anchors" for spiritual time. Use a certain candle, music, location, or physical position that signals to your brain it's time to focus on God. Sensory cues help ADHD brains transition into different modes.

When Jesus corrected Martha for being "worried and upset about many things," He wasn't criticizing her service or her concern for hospitality. He was pointing out that her attention was scattered across too many concerns simultaneously, preventing her from being fully present to what mattered most in that moment. Mary had chosen to focus her attention on "one thing"—being present with Jesus—and that focus gave her access to something valuable that couldn't be taken away.

An environment that supports focus requires intentional design. This might mean turning off all notifications during Bible study, using website blockers during prayer time, or keeping your phone in another room when you're trying to concentrate. Your environment either supports your attention or sabotages it. There's rarely a neutral middle ground.

The concept of "attention residue" explains why your mind feels cluttered even when you're trying to focus on spiritual things. When you quickly check your email before prayer, part of your attention remains stuck on work concerns. When you scroll through social media before Bible study, part of your mental bandwidth is still processing information from your feeds. Creating transition rituals can help clear this mental clutter and prepare your brain for focused spiritual engagement.

Hyperfocus can become a powerful spiritual tool when directed intentionally. When you find yourself naturally hyperfocusing on Scripture study, prayer, or ministry work, lean into it instead of fighting it. These states of intense concentration often produce profound spiritual insights and deep connection with God. The key is recognizing when hyperfocus is happening and protecting that time from interruption.

Hyperfocus also has a shadow side. You might become so absorbed in studying one biblical topic that you neglect other areas of spiritual growth. You might hyperfocus on serving others while neglecting your own spiritual needs. You might get lost in theological rabbit trails while missing practical applications. Learning to recognize when hyperfocus is productive versus when it's become unhealthy obsession is crucial for spiritual balance.

> ✘ **Danger Zone:** Don't attempt to eliminate all distractions from your environment. Your ADHD brain needs some stimulation to function optimally, and trying to create perfect silence often creates more distraction through the effort to maintain it.

The paradox of ADHD attention is that you often focus best when you're not trying to focus. This sounds counterintuitive, but forced concentration creates internal pressure that interferes with natural attention flow. Instead of gritting your teeth and trying to focus harder, experiment with gentle awareness. Notice when your mind wanders, acknowledge the distraction without judgment, and gently return your attention to your intended focus.

Movement can be your friend in developing sustained attention. Walking prayers, pacing while reading Scripture, or fidgeting with something tactile while listening to sermons can help regulate your attention instead of fighting it. The key is finding the right amount of movement—enough to help your brain settle but not so much that it becomes its own distraction.

Visual focus techniques can help anchor scattered attention. Instead of trying to maintain abstract concentration, give your eyes something to focus on: a cross, a picture, words on a page, or even a simple dot on the wall. Visual anchors provide external structure for internal attention and can help prevent mental wandering.

Time-boxing can make overwhelming spiritual practices feel manageable. Instead of committing to hour-long prayer sessions that feel impossible to maintain, try five-minute focused prayer blocks. Set a timer, focus completely for that short period, then take a break. These brief periods of intense focus can be more spiritually productive than longer periods of scattered attention.

The pomodoro technique adapts well to spiritual disciplines. Twenty-five minutes of focused Bible study followed by a five-minute break often works better than trying to maintain concentration for extended periods. Your brain needs regular rest intervals to maintain attention, and fighting this natural rhythm usually backfires.

Technology can be either your biggest enemy or your most helpful tool for managing attention. Apps that block distracting websites, timers that create structure, and white noise that masks environmental distractions can all support focus. But technology can also fragment your attention through notifications, infinite scrolling, and dopamine-driven design. The key is being intentional about which technologies you invite into your spiritual life and which ones you keep out.

Attention training through meditation and mindfulness practices can help strengthen your ability to notice when your mind wanders and gently redirect it. These practices need modification for ADHD brains. Traditional meditation instructions to "clear your mind" or "focus on nothing" can be frustrating and counterproductive. Instead, try focused attention meditation where you concentrate on something concrete: your breath, a Scripture verse, or a prayer phrase.

The spiritual practice of presence requires accepting your current attention state without judgment. Some days your mind will be scattered and unfocused. Other days you'll have laser-sharp concentration. Both states can be opportunities for spiritual growth if you approach them with grace instead of self-criticism. God doesn't love you more on focused days and less on scattered days.

Learning to pray scattered prayers can be as spiritually valuable as maintaining sustained concentration. Quick prayers throughout the day, sentence prayers between tasks, and even prayer fragments that get interrupted can all be meaningful communication with God. David's psalms weren't all sustained theological meditations. Some were brief cries for help, expressions of gratitude, or moments of worship scattered throughout his day.

The guilt and shame that often accompany attention struggles can become spiritual obstacles in themselves. When you feel frustrated about your scattered spiritual life, that frustration becomes another distraction pulling your attention away from God. Learning to accept your attention patterns with grace and work with them creatively is often more spiritually productive than fighting them with willpower.

Attentional stamina builds gradually through consistent practice, not through heroic efforts that lead to burnout. Start with very short periods of focused spiritual activity and gradually increase the duration as your attention strengthens. Think of it like physical fitness—you wouldn't start a workout program by trying to run a marathon on the first day.

Jesus often withdrew from crowds and distractions to pray in solitary places. He understood the importance of creating environments that supported focused communion with the Father. Following His example might mean being more selective about when, where, and how you engage in spiritual practices, choosing quality of attention over quantity of time.

> ✗ **Danger Zone:** Avoid comparing your attention span to neurotypical Christians or spiritual "giants." Their brains work differently than yours, and their practices might not translate to your neurological reality.

Your scattered attention isn't a spiritual defect. It's a different way of processing information and engaging with the world. The goal isn't to develop neurotypical focus patterns but to learn how to channel your unique attention style in ways that deepen your relationship with God and align with His purposes for your life. Some of the most creative spiritual insights and innovative ministry approaches come from minds that don't think in straight lines.

Working with your attention instead of against it transforms both your spiritual practices and your relationship with God. When you stop fighting your brain's design and start honoring its patterns, you discover that your supposed attention problems might be doorways to deeper spiritual experiences than conventional approaches could provide.

Emotional Regulation and RSD (Rejection Sensitive Dysphoria)

The email was innocuous enough: "Hey, can we chat about your presentation tomorrow? I have a few suggestions." But your heart immediately starts racing. Your stomach drops. Your mind begins catastrophizing: They hated it. I'm going to get fired. Everyone thinks I'm incompetent. I should never have volunteered for this project. Within minutes, you've spiraled from a simple request for feedback into a full-blown emotional crisis.

Welcome to life with Rejection Sensitive Dysphoria (RSD), one of the most painful and misunderstood aspects of ADHD. RSD isn't just being sensitive to criticism. It's an intense, overwhelming emotional reaction to perceived rejection, criticism, or failure that feels like being stabbed in the chest. For many ADHD Christians, RSD makes church environments treacherous because any correction, suggestion, or even well-meaning advice can trigger shame spirals that last for days.

RSD develops as a protective mechanism after years of criticism and misunderstanding. If you grew up hearing "try harder," "pay attention," "sit still," and "why can't you be more like your sister," your brain learned to scan constantly for signs of disapproval. The same neural pathways that make you emotionally intense also make you hypervigilant to rejection. You become an expert at reading facial expressions, voice tones, and body language, always watching for the slightest hint that someone is disappointed in you.

Fourth grade. Square dancing. The teacher announced it with forced enthusiasm, and what followed was social execution disguised as education: girls picked boys one by one until everyone was matched. I stood against the wall and watched my classmates pair off, my stomach sinking with each selection that wasn't me.

I was the last one chosen. Of course.

"Ha! Richard gets to dance with the ugliest girl in school because he's the ugliest boy!" The voice came from across the room, loud enough for everyone to hear.

The teacher heard it. She saw my face. She did nothing — just smiled and told us to get into position.

That moment created a permanent aversion that lasted decades. I never danced again — not at weddings, not at parties, nowhere. My body had logged the equation with perfect clarity: social participation equals public risk of degradation, and the adults in charge are fine with that outcome.

RSD works exactly like this. It doesn't develop in a vacuum. It builds from a lifetime of incidents where your brain — already wired for emotional intensity — experienced genuine pain and learned to anticipate it everywhere. When you flinch at mild criticism or read rejection into a neutral email, you're not being irrational. You're running threat-detection software that was calibrated by real experience. Understanding that is the first step toward recalibrating it.

> ⚠ **Caution:** Avoid immediately apologizing or people-pleasing when you suspect RSD is active. Take time to assess whether you did anything wrong before taking responsibility for others' reactions.

This hypervigilance extends into your spiritual life in devastating ways. When the pastor mentions the importance of consistency in your walk with God, you don't hear general teaching. You hear personal condemnation for your scattered spiritual life. When a small group leader suggests better time management, you don't hear helpful advice. You hear confirmation that you're a spiritual failure. When someone offers to pray for your struggles, you don't hear compassion. You hear pity for how broken you are.

I know this from the inside. There's a specific kind of sermon — the ones about sin, about hell, about how we all fall short — that my RSD turned into a personal address. The pastor wasn't looking at me. He was talking to a room of two hundred people. My nervous system didn't care. By the third sentence I was already certain he was describing me specifically, that everyone around me could tell, and that I had no business being there.

I left. Didn't say anything to anyone. Just got up and walked out while the sermon was still going.

That was years ago. I still haven't gone back to that church.

The spiral didn't start because the theology was wrong or the pastor was cruel. It started because a brain wired for rejection sensitivity sat in a room where the message was 'you are a sinner' and heard 'you, specifically, are the problem.' RSD doesn't distinguish between a general truth and a personal attack. It processes both the same way.

If you've walked out of a sermon and driven home in a cold rage you couldn't fully explain, this is why. If you've stopped going to a church — or stopped going to church altogether — after a message that everyone else seemed to receive as encouragement, this is why. You weren't being dramatic or thin-skinned. Your nervous system was doing exactly what years of criticism trained it to do.

The practical implication: you may need to choose churches and pastors carefully based not just on theology but on preaching style. A pastor who leads primarily through guilt and conviction — even accurate, well-intentioned guilt and conviction — may be functionally inaccessible to you regardless of how sound the doctrine is. That's not spiritual immaturity. It's knowing your nervous system.

The church's emphasis on sanctification and spiritual growth can become a minefield for RSD. Messages about dying to self, taking every thought captive, and walking in the Spirit get filtered through a brain that's already convinced it's not measuring up. You hear calls to holiness as indictments of your messiness. You interpret teaching on self-control as criticism of your impulsivity. You receive encouragement to "be transformed" as evidence that your current self is unacceptable.

But here's what's remarkable about RSD: the same emotional intensity that makes criticism feel devastating also gives you extraordinary empathy and compassion. You can sense when someone is hurting because your brain is constantly monitoring emotional cues. You feel others' pain deeply because your emotional system operates at high volume. You respond with immediate compassion because you know what it feels like to be wounded.

This emotional sensitivity isn't a bug in your spiritual operating system. It's a feature that enables deep connection with God and others. David, who wrote many of the most emotionally intense psalms, understood this. His writings reveal someone who felt everything deeply: joy, sorrow, anger, fear, love, and despair. Psalm 34:18 speaks directly to your experience: "The Lord is close to the brokenhearted and saves those who are crushed in spirit." God doesn't distance Himself from emotional intensity. He draws near to it.

The challenge isn't to eliminate emotional intensity but to learn healthy ways to regulate and channel it. Emotional regulation for ADHD brains looks different from neurotypical approaches. Traditional advice like "count to ten" or "think before you react" assumes you have the executive function to pause and process in the moment. Your brain often bypasses the prefrontal cortex and goes straight into fight-or-flight mode when triggered.

Knowing your emotional triggers is the first step toward regulation. RSD often activates in response to criticism of your work, correction of your behavior, exclusion from social activities, or failure to meet expectations. Knowing your triggers helps you prepare for them and develop coping strategies before you're in crisis mode.

Physical regulation strategies can be more effective than cognitive ones when you're emotionally dysregulated. Deep breathing, progressive muscle relaxation, cold water on your face, or vigorous exercise can help reset your nervous system faster than trying to think your way out of an emotional spiral. Your body needs to calm down before your mind can engage rational thought.

The "STOP" technique can provide a framework for emotional regulation: Stop what you're doing, Take a breath, Observe what you're feeling, and Proceed with intention. For ADHD brains, this might need modification. Instead of trying to analyze your emotions in the moment, focus on physical regulation first. Stop, breathe deeply, move your body, then think about what happened.

Space between trigger and response takes planning and practice. When you receive criticism or correction, you might need to buy yourself time: "Thank you for the feedback. Let me think about this and get back to you." This gives your emotional system time to regulate before you respond in ways you'll regret later.

> ★ **Pro Tip:** Create an "RSD emergency kit" with scripture verses, worship songs, contact info for safe people, and grounding exercises. Keep it easily accessible on your phone or printed somewhere you can find it when you're dysregulated.

The spiritual practice of lament can be healing for ADHD Christians struggling with RSD. The Psalms are full of emotional outpouring to God: complaints, anger, confusion, and despair. David didn't sanitize his emotions before bringing them to God. He brought his raw, intense feelings directly into his relationship with the Almighty. Psalm 13 begins with "How long, Lord? Will you forget me forever?" This isn't lack of faith. This is honest emotional engagement with God.

Learning to recognize the difference between shame and conviction is crucial for spiritual health. The Holy Spirit's conviction feels targeted, hopeful, and productive. It points toward behaviors or attitudes that need to change and provides clear direction for growth. Shame feels global, hopeless, and destructive. It tells you that you're fundamentally flawed and beyond redemption.

When RSD gets triggered in church contexts, shame often masquerades as spiritual conviction. A sermon on anger makes you feel terrible about your emotional outbursts, but instead of receiving guidance for growth, you spiral into general self-condemnation. Learning to pause and ask "Is this conviction leading me toward change, or is this shame telling me I'm worthless?" can help you discern the source of your emotional response.

Rejection Sensitive Dysphoria can also manifest as people-pleasing, perfectionism, or conflict avoidance. You might overcommit to church activities to prove your worth, avoid expressing disagreement to prevent rejection, or work frantically to meet impossible standards. These coping mechanisms feel protective in the moment but ultimately reinforce the belief that your authentic self is unacceptable.

The antidote to RSD isn't thicker skin or emotional numbness. It's learning to ground your identity in God's unchanging love instead of others' approval. Romans 8:38-39 declares that nothing can separate you from the love of Christ. This isn't just theological truth. It's practical medicine for the RSD-wounded soul. When someone's criticism triggers your shame spiral, you can return to this anchor: God's love for you doesn't fluctuate based on your performance or others' opinions.

★ **Pro Tip:** Practice the "24-hour rule" for RSD episodes. Don't make major decisions, send important emails, or have crucial conversations until at least 24 hours after an RSD trigger. Your perception is temporarily distorted and needs time to recalibrate.

A theology of imperfection becomes essential for ADHD Christians. The gospel message isn't that you need to get your act together before God will love you. It's that God loves you while you're still a mess and is committed to the long, slow process of transformation. Your emotional dysregulation, impulsivity, and scattered attention don't disqualify you from God's love. They're part of the raw material He's working with.

Emotional resilience requires recognizing that other people's opinions about you aren't necessarily true or important. When someone criticizes your ministry approach, that doesn't mean you're called to quit serving. When a church member makes a comment about your parenting, that doesn't mean you're a terrible parent. When a friend seems distant, that doesn't mean they hate you. Learning to reality-test your emotional reactions can prevent minor interactions from becoming major crises.

The practice of self-compassion becomes crucial for managing RSD. When you make a mistake or receive criticism, instead of launching into self-attack mode, try responding to yourself the way you would respond to a good friend in the same situation. What would you say to encourage them? How would you help them put the situation in perspective? This isn't making excuses or avoiding responsibility. It's treating yourself with the same kindness and understanding you'd offer others.

Finding safe people who understand your emotional intensity without trying to fix or minimize it is essential for healing from RSD. These might be other neurodivergent Christians, mental health professionals who understand ADHD, or simply friends who've learned to accept your emotional patterns without judgment. Having people in your life who can provide reality checks during shame spirals can prevent RSD episodes from escalating.

★ **Pro Tip:** Develop "rejection reality checks" with trusted friends. When RSD hits, text someone who knows you well with the situation and ask, "Does this sound like real rejection or RSD?" An outside perspective can break the emotional spiral.

Sometimes professional help is necessary for managing severe RSD. Therapy can provide tools for emotional regulation, medication can help stabilize mood swings, and support groups can offer community with others who understand your experience. There's no shame in seeking professional help for emotional struggles any more than there would be shame in seeing a doctor for a broken bone.

Learning to set boundaries becomes crucial for protecting your emotional well-being. This might mean limiting time with people who consistently trigger your RSD, leaving situations when you feel overwhelmed, or being selective about the feedback you seek. Boundaries aren't walls that keep everyone out. They're gates that let in what's helpful and keep out what's harmful.

The goal isn't to become emotionally invulnerable. The goal is to learn to feel deeply without being destroyed by those feelings. Your emotional intensity is part of how God designed you to experience life and connect with others. The challenge is learning to steward that intensity in healthy ways that promote growth instead of shame.

Remember that emotional regulation is a skill that improves with practice, not a character trait you either have or lack. Every time you successfully manage an RSD episode, you're building emotional muscle memory. Every time you choose self-compassion over self-attack, you're rewiring neural pathways. Every time you reach out for support instead of isolating, you're strengthening your emotional resilience.

✗ **Danger Zone:** Avoid isolating yourself from church community because of RSD fears. The very relationships you're afraid will reject you are often the ones that provide the most healing, but you have to risk connection to receive it.

Your intense emotions aren't evidence of spiritual immaturity. They're evidence of a heart that feels deeply and a brain that processes intensely. God didn't make a mistake when He gave you this emotional operating system. He gave you the capacity for profound empathy, passionate worship, and deep connection with others. Learning to regulate and channel these emotions is part of becoming the person He designed you to be.

Masking, Authenticity, and Social Struggles

"The Lord does not look at the things people look at. People look at the outward appearance, but the Lord looks at the heart." (1 Samuel 16:7, NIV)

"Therefore each of you must put off falsehood and speak truthfully to your neighbor, for we are all members of one body." (Ephesians 4:25, NIV)

You're at a church potluck, standing in the corner with a plate of food you're not eating, watching everyone else navigate conversations with apparent ease. You've been here for an hour, and you've had maybe three meaningful interactions. The rest of the time has been spent performing what you think of as "normal person" behavior: smiling at appropriate moments, nodding along to conversations you can't quite follow, and suppressing the urge to interrupt with tangential thoughts that seem fascinating to you but probably wouldn't land well with this crowd.

Your face hurts from maintaining the pleasant expression. Your energy is depleted from constantly monitoring your behavior, volume, and body language. You've caught yourself about to share an overly personal story twice, stopped yourself from making a joke that might be misunderstood, and redirected three conversations away from topics that genuinely interest you because they seem too intense for casual social interaction.

By the time you get home, you're completely drained. You've spent so much energy being the person you thought everyone else wanted you to be that you've forgotten who you are underneath the performance. This exhausting dance between your authentic self and your socially acceptable self has become so automatic that you barely notice it anymore. But the cost accumulates: loneliness, disconnection, and a growing sense that nobody really knows or likes the real you.

Masking is the process of camouflaging your natural ADHD traits to appear more socially acceptable. It's suppressing your impulses, moderating your enthusiasm, hiding your struggles, and performing neurotypical behavior patterns that don't come naturally to your brain.

★ **Pro Tip:** Gradually unmask in low-stakes relationships before attempting authenticity in high-pressure situations. Practice vulnerability in safe spaces to build confidence for riskier contexts where being real feels more dangerous.

You learned to mask early. Probably by age seven. Too much, too loud, too intense — the feedback was relentless. Sit still. Think before you speak. Dial it down. You got very good at performing a version of yourself that other people could tolerate. Gradually, you developed an elaborate system of self-monitoring and self-correction designed to help you fit in.

Masking might involve forcing yourself to make eye contact even when it feels overwhelming, sitting still when your body wants to move, keeping your voice at an acceptable volume when excitement makes you want to shout, or pretending to follow conversations when your mind has wandered to more interesting topics. It's laughing at jokes you don't find funny, showing interest in subjects that bore you, and hiding the things you're genuinely passionate about because they don't seem socially appropriate.

The Christian community can be challenging for ADHD masking because there are often unspoken expectations about how believers should behave. You're supposed to be patient, gentle, self-controlled, and consistent. You're expected to sit quietly through long services, engage in small talk at social events, and serve faithfully in organized ministries. When your natural traits don't align with these expectations, masking becomes a survival strategy for remaining part of the community.

★ **Pro Tip:** Develop a "masking energy budget" to track how much emotional labor you can sustain. Just like physical energy, social performance energy is finite and needs conscious management and recovery time.

Jesus said His yoke is easy and His burden is light. If your Christian life feels like an exhausting performance where you can never let your guard down, you might be carrying a yoke that He never intended for you. The burden of constant masking is heavy, not light. The anxiety of perpetual self-monitoring is hard, not easy. God's acceptance isn't contingent on your ability to act neurotypical.

Samuel's reminder that "the Lord looks at the heart" while "people look at the outward appearance" speaks directly to the masking dilemma. Other people might judge you based on whether you conform to social expectations, but God sees and loves your authentic self. The traits you're working so hard to hide or modify aren't flaws in His design. They're features He intentionally included in your personality and purpose.

Masking creates a painful split between your public and private selves. In public, you're performing an acceptable version of yourself that follows social scripts and meets behavioral expectations. In private, you can finally relax into your natural patterns, but you might feel guilty about the discrepancy or worry that people would reject you if they saw your unmasked self.

This split can lead to identity confusion and imposter syndrome. You might not be sure which version of yourself is "real" or worry that you're being deceptive by presenting differently in social situations. The truth is that both versions are you—one is just filtered through social anxiety and performance pressure while the other is more natural and authentic.

The exhaustion that comes from masking is real and significant. It takes tremendous mental energy to constantly monitor and modify your behavior. This cognitive load can deplete your resources for other tasks and leave you feeling drained after social interactions that seem effortless for others. You might need more recovery time after social events, not because you don't enjoy people, but because the energy required to mask is enormous.

Social struggles for ADHD brains often stem from differences in communication style, attention patterns, and emotional regulation that don't match neurotypical social norms. You might interrupt conversations because your brain processes thoughts faster than your impulse control can manage them. You might seem disinterested in small talk because your brain craves deeper, more stimulating discussions. You might appear self-centered because your enthusiasm for your interests overrides your ability to read social cues about when to stop talking.

These aren't character flaws or signs that you don't care about others. They're neurological differences that become social challenges when you're operating in environments designed for different brain types. Understanding this distinction can help reduce the shame and self-criticism that often accompany social difficulties.

Rejection Sensitive Dysphoria adds another layer of complexity to social interactions. Your brain interprets neutral expressions as signs of disapproval, delayed responses as evidence of rejection, and social corrections as devastating personal attacks. This hypersensitivity to social feedback can make you either withdraw from social situations entirely or increase your masking efforts to avoid any possibility of criticism.

The fear of being "found out" or having your mask slip can create constant anxiety in social situations. You might worry that people will notice you're different, that they'll realize you're not as socially competent as you're pretending to be, or that they'll reject you if they see your authentic self. This anxiety often becomes a self-fulfilling prophecy as the fear of social failure makes you more likely to say or do awkward things.

Learning to unmask safely requires finding people and environments where your authentic self is welcomed and appreciated. This might mean seeking out neurodivergent-friendly communities, joining groups centered around your genuine interests, or building relationships with people who value authenticity over conformity. Not everyone will appreciate your unmasked self, but the people who do are your real tribe.

The process of unmasking can feel terrifying because you've learned that your natural traits are socially unacceptable. You might worry that without your mask, you'll be rejected, criticized, or isolated. The paradox is that masking often prevents the deep connections you're seeking. When you hide your authentic self, you can't form authentic relationships. People can only love and accept the version of you that they're allowed to see.

Church communities have an opportunity to be places where masking isn't necessary, where people can "put off falsehood and speak truthfully" as Paul instructs in Ephesians 4:25. This means creating environments where neurodivergent traits are understood and appreciated, where social mistakes are met with grace instead of judgment, and where different types of engagement and participation are welcomed.

Many church environments inadvertently reinforce masking by emphasizing conformity, quiet behavior, and traditional forms of participation. When churches prioritize order and predictability over authenticity and inclusion, they can become places where ADHD people feel they must hide their true selves to belong.

> ✗ Danger Zone: Avoid churches or groups that demand conformity to neurotypical social norms as evidence of spiritual maturity. Your neurodivergent social style isn't less spiritual than neurotypical presentations — it's differently spiritual.

Social skills development as an ADHD adult requires a different approach than the one-size-fits-all advice typically offered. You need strategies that work with your brain patterns instead of against them. This might mean learning to pause before speaking, developing scripts for common social situations, or finding ways to channel your energy appropriately in group settings.

Skill development shouldn't be confused with masking. The goal isn't to become neurotypical but to learn how to navigate neurotypical social environments more effectively while still honoring your authentic self. This might mean asking for clarification when you miss social cues, explicitly stating your communication preferences, or taking breaks when social situations become overwhelming.

Genuine connections require vulnerability and the courage to let people see your real self. This doesn't mean oversharing or ignoring social boundaries, but it does mean being honest about your experiences, needs, and challenges. When you share your struggles with ADHD, you often discover that others have their own hidden challenges and that your openness gives them permission to be more authentic as well.

The concept of "selective unmasking" can be helpful for managing the risks and benefits of authenticity. You don't have to be equally open with everyone, but you can identify safe relationships and environments where you can gradually reduce your masking behaviors. This allows you to experience the relief and connection that come with authenticity while still protecting yourself in situations where masking might be necessary for safety or professional reasons.

Sensory overwhelm often contributes to social struggles for ADHD brains. Crowded, noisy environments can make it difficult to focus on conversations, process social information, or regulate your emotions effectively. Recognizing your sensory needs and advocating for accommodations (quieter spaces, shorter interactions, permission to take breaks) can make social situations more manageable.

The pressure to be consistently available and socially engaged can be overwhelming for ADHD brains that need more recovery time and have limited social energy. Learning to set boundaries around social commitments, communicate your availability honestly, and prioritize relationships that energize instead of drain you becomes essential for sustainable social connection.

Online communities can provide valuable spaces for authentic connection with other neurodivergent people who understand your experiences. These relationships can offer the acceptance and understanding that helps you maintain confidence in your authentic self even when you encounter rejection or misunderstanding in other contexts.

The goal isn't to eliminate all social adaptation or to ignore the impact of your behavior on others. Healthy relationships require mutual consideration and compromise. But this adaptation should come from a place of choice and care for others instead of fear and shame about your authentic self. When you adapt your behavior out of love instead of terror, it feels different and costs less energy.

> ★ Pro Tip: Create "authenticity anchors" — small ways to be genuinely yourself even in masking situations. This might be wearing something that reflects your personality, using humor that feels natural, or asking questions that genuinely interest you.

A theology of authenticity means understanding that God created you with intention and purpose, including the traits that feel socially challenging. Your ADHD brain isn't a mistake that needs to be hidden but a unique design that serves certain purposes in God's kingdom. When you mask your authentic self, you might be hiding gifts and perspectives that others need to see.

Jesus modeled authenticity throughout His ministry. He didn't conform to social expectations when they conflicted with His mission and values. He spoke truth even when it made people uncomfortable, expressed emotions openly, and built relationships with people who were marginalized by conventional society. His example gives us permission to be real instead of performing acceptability.

> ⚠ Caution: Don't abandon all social filtering in the name of authenticity. It doesn't mean saying everything you think to everyone you meet — it means being genuine within appropriate boundaries for each relationship and context.

The path toward authenticity is gradual and requires patience with yourself and others. You've spent years learning to mask, and unmasking safely takes time. Some relationships may not survive increased authenticity, but the ones that do will be deeper and more meaningful. Some environments may never feel safe for your authentic self, but you can find or create spaces where you can be real.

Your authentic self deserves to be known and loved. The energy you spend masking could be redirected toward relationships and activities that bring you joy and fulfillment. The isolation you feel when constantly performing can be replaced by genuine connection with people who appreciate your unique perspective and contributions.

God doesn't call you to be someone else. He calls you to be yourself—fully, authentically, courageously yourself. Your ADHD traits, your intense emotions, your scattered attention, your creative thinking, and your passionate engagement with life are all part of the person He created you to be. Learning to honor and express your authentic self isn't selfishness or rebellion. It's obedience to the God who made you exactly as you are for exactly the purposes He has in mind.

> ⚠ **Caution:** Avoid using authenticity as an excuse for social behaviors that consistently hurt others. Being genuine includes taking responsibility for your impact and making efforts to communicate in ways others can receive.

The world needs what you have to offer, but it can only benefit from your gifts if you have the courage to stop hiding them behind a mask of acceptability. Your authentic self might be inconvenient, intense, or unfamiliar to others, but it's also irreplaceable, valuable, and deeply loved by the One who created you to be precisely who you are.

Time, Organization, and Stewardship

"Be very careful, then, how you live—not as unwise but as wise, making the most of every opportunity, because the days are evil." (Ephesians 5:15-16, NIV)

"Do not boast about tomorrow, for you do not know what a day may bring." (Proverbs 27:1, NIV)

"Suppose one of you wants to build a tower. Won't you first sit down and estimate the cost to see if you have enough money to complete it?" (Luke 14:28, NIV)

It's 3:00 AM and you're lying in bed calculating how many hours of sleep you'll get if you fall asleep right now. Your mind is racing through tomorrow's to-do list, which somehow grew from three items this morning to seventeen items by bedtime. You forgot to call your mom back, you're not sure if you paid the electric bill, and you have a vague sense that you promised to do something important for someone but can't remember what or when.

You finally drift off to sleep around 4:30 AM, wake up at 7:00 AM feeling like you've been hit by a truck, and stumble through your morning routine fifteen minutes behind schedule. You arrive at work having forgotten your lunch, your phone charger, and the report you stayed up late finishing. By noon, you're overwhelmed, behind on everything, and wondering how other people make life look so effortless.

Welcome to time blindness, executive dysfunction, and the unique challenges of stewardship with an ADHD brain. You're not lazy, irresponsible, or spiritually immature. You're trying to manage time, tasks, and resources with a brain that processes these things differently from the neurotypical world around you.

Time blindness affects how you experience and estimate time passage. Five minutes can feel like an hour when you're bored, and three hours can disappear in what feels like twenty minutes when you're hyperfocused. You might think you have plenty of time to get ready for church and end up rushing out the door twenty minutes late. Or you might arrive thirty minutes early because you overcompensated for your usual lateness.

This isn't poor time management in the traditional sense. It's a neurological difference in how your brain processes temporal information. The same part of your brain that struggles with time awareness also struggles with working memory, planning, and task initiation. Understanding this removes the moral judgment from your time struggles and opens up possibilities for creative solutions.

The first time I understood that structure could work with my brain instead of against it, I was doing dishes.

I was maybe six or seven. My mother handed me a dish towel and explained the system: scrape, rinse, she washes, I dry, stack. My father stood in the doorway watching. I asked why I had to do it. He said one dollar and twenty-five cents a week, and you earn it. I wanted to argue. I had a Lego spaceship waiting on my bedroom floor.

But then something unexpected happened. The rhythm settled in. Scrape, rinse, dry, squeak, stack. My breath matched the motion. The kitchen calmed. The part of my brain that usually needed to be somewhere else found something to hold onto — a sequence with a clear start and a visible end. By the time I tied off the trash bag, I felt something I didn't have a word for: the small, clean satisfaction of done.

That's what ADHD brains are chasing when we hyperfocus, when we build elaborate systems, when we turn everything into a collection or a project with measurable progress. We're chasing that feeling of rhythm clicking into place. The problem isn't that we can't organize. It's that standard organizational advice assumes a brain that finds structure naturally motivating. Ours needs the rhythm to be built in — visible, physical, immediate, and tied to something that feels real.

Paul's instruction to "make the most of every opportunity" wasn't written to people with smartphones, digital calendars, and competing demands for every moment of their day. He was writing to believers who lived in a simpler but still challenging world. The principle of wise stewardship remains timeless, but the application needs to account for how your ADHD brain experiences and manages time.

> ⚠ **Caution:** Avoid complex organizational systems that require daily maintenance. Your ADHD brain will abandon them during stressful periods, creating more shame and chaos than the original disorganization.

Traditional time management advice assumes you have consistent executive function, reliable working memory, and the ability to estimate how long tasks will take. These assumptions don't hold for ADHD brains. You might forget about commitments five minutes after making them, underestimate how long projects will take by factors of two or three, and struggle to break large tasks into manageable steps.

The solution isn't trying harder or developing more discipline. It's building external systems that compensate for internal executive function challenges. Your brain needs scaffolding—external structures that support internal processes that don't work reliably on their own.

The calendar isn't a scheduling tool. It's your external brain. Everything goes in it: appointments, bill deadlines, reminders to call your mother, personal care prompts. If it's not in the calendar, it doesn't exist — not because you don't care, but because your working memory has other things going on. This isn't over-scheduling. It's survival.

Time-blocking can help translate abstract time concepts into concrete visual representations. Instead of just writing "work on project" in your calendar, block out two hours from 9:00 to

11:00 AM for project work. This helps your brain understand how much time you're committing and prevents you from overcommitting your schedule.

The planning fallacy affects ADHD brains more severely than neurotypical ones. You consistently underestimate how long tasks will take because your brain doesn't account for all the steps involved. A simple solution is the "multiply by three" rule: whatever time you think something will take, multiply by three. This isn't pessimism. It's realistic planning that accounts for your brain's optimistic time estimates.

Buffer time becomes crucial for managing the unexpected delays and attention shifts that are part of ADHD life. If you have an appointment at 2:00 PM, don't schedule anything for 1:45 PM. Build in cushions that allow for traffic, forgotten items, or getting distracted by something urgent on your way out the door.

Organization systems need to be simple, visible, and sustainable. Complex filing systems that work for neurotypical brains often become overwhelming clutter for ADHD brains. The key is finding the minimum viable organization that prevents important things from getting lost without creating maintenance overhead that becomes its own source of stress.

The "one-touch rule" can prevent small tasks from becoming overwhelming piles. When you pick up a piece of mail, either deal with it immediately, put it in a designated action pile, or throw it away. Don't set it down "just for now" because "just for now" often becomes "lost forever" with ADHD brains.

Visual organization works better than hidden organization for most ADHD minds. Clear containers, open shelving, and labeled systems help you remember what you have and where you put it. If you can't see it, it doesn't exist. This applies to both physical spaces and digital organization.

Money management presents unique challenges for ADHD brains because it combines time awareness, impulse control, and executive function. You might forget to pay bills, make impulsive purchases, or lose track of spending. The emotional dysregulation that comes with ADHD can also lead to retail therapy or anxiety-driven spending.

Automatic systems can remove executive function from financial stewardship. Set up automatic bill payments, automatic savings transfers, and automatic investing contributions. This prevents important financial tasks from depending on your memory or motivation. You can still maintain oversight and control while reducing the cognitive load of managing these systems manually.

The envelope method adapts well to ADHD money management. Whether you use physical cash envelopes or digital equivalents, having predetermined spending categories with clear limits can prevent impulsive overspending. When the envelope is empty, you're done spending in that category until next month.

Impulse control strategies become essential for faithful stewardship. The 24-hour rule for non-essential purchases gives your brain time to move past the initial impulse. Add items to a wish list instead of buying them immediately. Often, the desire passes once the initial emotional excitement fades.

Biblical stewardship includes managing your energy and attention, not just your time and money. Your ADHD brain has limited executive function resources that get depleted throughout the day. Learning to budget these mental resources is as important as budgeting financial resources.

> ✖ **Danger Zone:** Avoid comparing your organizational abilities to neurotypical Christians. Their brains process information and maintain systems differently than yours, and their methods might make your challenges worse.

Decision fatigue affects ADHD brains more severely than neurotypical ones. Making too many decisions depletes your mental energy and leads to poor choices later in the day. Reducing unnecessary decisions through routines, templates, and predetermined choices preserves mental energy for more important decisions.

The concept of "good enough" becomes a spiritual discipline for perfectionist ADHD minds. Trying to optimize every decision and perfect every system can become a form of idolatry that prevents you from focusing on what matters most. Sometimes the best stewardship choice is to accept an 80% solution so you can move on to other important things.

Delegation and outsourcing can be wise stewardship when they free you to focus on your unique gifts and calling. If you struggle with organization, hiring a cleaner might be better stewardship than spending hours every week fighting clutter. If you struggle with financial details, working with a financial advisor might be better stewardship than trying to manage everything yourself.

The parable of the talents teaches about faithful stewardship of gifts and resources, but it doesn't specify what that stewardship must look like. The servant who doubled his talents might have used different methods than the servant who earned five more. Your stewardship methods need to match your brain's design, not someone else's template.

Technology can be a powerful stewardship tool when used intentionally. Apps that track spending, remind you of deadlines, or automate routine tasks can compensate for executive function challenges. Technology can also become a distraction that undermines stewardship if not used thoughtfully.

> ★ **Pro Tip:** Automate financial stewardship wherever possible. Set up automatic transfers to savings and giving accounts so stewardship happens even when executive function is offline. Your future dysregulated self will thank your current organized self.

The Sabbath principle becomes important for ADHD brains that tend toward either obsessive hyperfocus or scattered overcommitment. Regular rest isn't laziness. It's faithful stewardship of the brain and body God gave you. Your executive function needs time to recharge, and your attention needs time to reset.

Saying no becomes a crucial stewardship skill when your brain naturally wants to say yes to everything interesting. Every commitment you make is a stewardship decision about how to use your limited time, energy, and attention. Learning to evaluate opportunities against your priorities and capacity prevents overcommitment that leads to poor performance in everything.

The planning fallacy applies to commitments as much as tasks. You might agree to help with three different ministry projects because each one seems manageable in isolation. When they all hit the same busy season, you're overwhelmed and can't do any of them well. Learning to think systemically about your commitments helps prevent this trap.

Seasonal approaches to stewardship can work better than trying to maintain perfect balance year-round. Some seasons might be intensive work periods. Others might focus on relationships or spiritual growth. Others might be rest and recovery periods. This rhythm reflects how ADHD brains naturally cycle through different levels of energy and focus.

The key to faithful stewardship with an ADHD brain is working with your neurological design instead of fighting against it. This might mean using timers instead of relying on internal time awareness, creating visual reminders instead of depending on memory, or building automatic systems instead of relying on consistent willpower.

Your stewardship doesn't have to look like anyone else's to be faithful. The goal isn't perfect organization or optimal efficiency. The goal is managing the resources God has entrusted to you in ways that honor Him and serve His purposes. This might look messy and unconventional to outside observers, but if it works for your brain and serves God's kingdom, it's faithful stewardship.

Stewardship is ultimately about trust and faithfulness, not performance and perfection. God knows how He designed your brain, and He's not expecting you to manage time, money, and resources like someone with different neurological wiring. He's expecting you to be faithful with what He's given you, using the brain He created to serve His purposes in the world.

Learning to steward your ADHD brain well is itself an act of worship. When you create systems that work with your design instead of against it, you're honoring the Creator who made you exactly as you are. When you find ways to use your unique gifts effectively, you're being faithful with the talents He's entrusted to you. When you manage your resources in ways that serve others and advance His kingdom, you're living out the calling He's placed on your life.

"Be kind and compassionate to one another, forgiving each other, just as in Christ God forgave you." (Ephesians 4:32, NIV)

"My dear brothers and sisters, take note of this: Everyone should be quick to listen, slow to speak and slow to become angry." (James 1:19, NIV)

You're in the middle of what you think is a pleasant conversation when you notice your friend's expression change. Their smile looks forced now, and they're giving shorter responses. You replay the last few minutes in your mind and realize you've been talking nonstop about your latest obsession for the past twenty minutes. You interrupted them three times when they tried to speak. You completely missed their subtle attempts to change the subject.

The familiar wave of shame washes over you. You've done it again. Despite your best intentions to be a good friend, listener, and conversational partner, your ADHD brain hijacked the interaction. You want to apologize, but you're not sure if acknowledging it will make things better or worse. So you awkwardly try to shift into listening mode, but now you're so anxious about your social performance that you can't focus on what they're saying.

You care deeply about people, sometimes to the point of emotional overwhelm. You want to connect authentically and love well. The very traits that make you passionate and empathetic can also make relationships challenging. The impulsivity that drives you to spontaneous acts of generosity can also lead to interrupting, oversharing, or saying things you later regret.

> ★ **Pro Tip:** Tell close friends and family about your ADHD symptoms before conflicts arise, not during them. Explain how your brain works during calm moments so they understand your behavior during heated ones. Education prevents misunderstandings.

James's instruction to be "quick to listen, slow to speak and slow to become angry" assumes you have the executive function to pause between impulse and action. Your ADHD brain often processes thoughts and emotions faster than your self-regulation can manage them. By the time you realize you should have listened more and talked less, the words are already out of your mouth.

This doesn't mean you're doomed to poor relationships. It means you need different strategies that work with your brain's design instead of against it. The goal isn't to become neurotypical in your communication style. It's to learn how to channel your natural intensity, enthusiasm, and emotional engagement in ways that build connection instead of creating distance.

Your emotional intensity is both a relationship superpower and a potential pitfall. When someone you care about is hurting, you feel their pain deeply and respond with immediate compassion. When you're excited about something, your enthusiasm can be contagious and inspiring. When you love someone, you love them with your whole heart. This same emotional intensity can also lead to overwhelming others with your feelings, taking things too personally, or reacting strongly to minor social cues.

The key is recognizing when your emotional volume is too high for the situation. Not suppressing it — modulating it. Enough to stay in the conversation without taking the roof off. This might mean taking a breath before responding to emotional triggers, asking for time to process before having difficult conversations, or learning to express intense feelings in ways that don't overwhelm the other person.

> ★ **Pro Tip:** Develop "repair scripts" for common ADHD-related relationship mistakes. "I interrupted you because my brain got excited about what you were saying, not because I don't value your thoughts" saves time and prevents repetitive explanations.

Rejection Sensitive Dysphoria adds another layer of complexity to relationships. You might interpret neutral expressions as disapproval, read rejection into delayed responses to texts, or assume that minor conflicts mean the relationship is over. This hypersensitivity to social cues can lead to constant anxiety about whether people like you and whether you're saying or doing the right things.

Learning to reality-test your emotional reactions becomes crucial for relationship health. When you feel that stab of rejection, pause and ask yourself: "Is there evidence that this person is rejecting me, or is my RSD being triggered by something neutral?" Often, what feels like clear signs of disapproval are just normal variations in people's moods, energy levels, or attention.

Timing matters more than you think. You might have important things to say at moments when the other person isn't ready to hear them. Learning to recognize when someone is available for deeper conversation versus when they need lighter interaction can prevent you from overwhelming them with intensity when they're not prepared for it.

The impulse to share everything immediately can strain relationships, especially romantic ones. Your brain might connect today's conversation to seventeen related topics, three personal anecdotes, and a funny video you saw last week. Before you know it, you've taken a simple question about dinner plans and turned it into a forty-minute monologue about your childhood, your work stress, and your theories about restaurant psychology.

Pausing before you share — asking whether this is the right moment and the right amount — is a skill, not suppression. It's the difference between authentic connection and information dumping. Your thoughts are worth sharing. Timing them well makes people more likely to actually receive them.

Interrupting damages relationships even when your intentions are good. Your brain knows this. It just can't always stop in time. It processes information quickly and makes connections you want to share before you forget them. Interrupting sends the message that what you have to say is more important than what the other person is saying, even when that's not what you mean.

> ★ **Pro Tip:** Use "echo listening" to combat ADHD attention issues in conversations. Repeat back what someone just said in your own words to ensure you heard them correctly and to show you're engaged even when your brain is scattered.

Physical strategies can help manage the impulse to interrupt. Try holding a small object that you can squeeze when you have something to say but need to wait your turn. Or jot down quick notes about what you want to contribute so you don't forget your thoughts while listening. These tools help bridge the gap between your fast-moving thoughts and your slower impulse control.

Hyperfocus can affect relationships in both positive and negative ways. When you hyperfocus on someone you care about, you can be incredibly attentive, remembering small details about their life and showing deep interest in their thoughts and feelings. Hyperfocus can also lead to intensity that feels overwhelming, especially in new relationships where the other person isn't prepared for that level of attention.

Learning to recognize when you're hyperfocusing on a relationship and checking in with the other person about whether that intensity feels good to them can prevent relationships from becoming unbalanced. Some people love being the focus of intense attention. Others find it overwhelming or smothering.

The flip side of hyperfocus is distractibility, which can make people feel ignored or unimportant even when you care about them deeply. You might be in the middle of a meaningful conversation when something catches your attention and your focus shifts completely. This can be hurtful to the other person, especially if it happens repeatedly.

Being aware of your attention patterns and communicating about them can help others understand that your distractibility isn't about them. A simple "I'm really interested in what you're saying, but I'm having trouble focusing right now. Can we continue this conversation later when I can give you my full attention?" acknowledges the issue without making excuses.

Time management challenges affect relationships when you're consistently late, forget important dates, or struggle to follow through on commitments. These issues can feel like lack of care or respect to others, even when they're executive function challenges instead of relationship priorities.

Being honest about your time management struggles and building systems to compensate for them can prevent these issues from damaging relationships. This might mean setting phone alarms for important calls, putting anniversaries and birthdays in your calendar with advance reminders, or asking for help remembering commitments that matter to people you care about.

Emotional regulation challenges can create relationship turbulence when you have strong reactions to minor issues or struggle to manage anger, disappointment, or frustration in healthy ways. Your emotions are valid and real, but expressing them in ways that damage relationships isn't helpful for anyone involved.

Learning to take breaks when you're emotionally escalated can prevent you from saying or doing things you'll regret later. A simple "I'm feeling really strongly about this right now and I don't want to say something hurtful. Can we take a break and come back to this in an hour?" can protect both you and the other person from emotional damage.

Boundary setting becomes crucial for managing the intensity that comes with ADHD relationships. You might need to limit how much emotional support you provide to others because your empathy can lead to taking on more than you can handle. You might need to ask for certain types of support from others during difficult times. You might need to communicate about what kinds of feedback you can receive and when.

These boundaries aren't selfish or uncaring. They're necessary for sustainable, healthy relationships. When you operate within your capacity and communicate your needs clearly, you can be more consistently available and supportive to the people you care about.

> ⚠ **Caution:** Don't use ADHD as an excuse for repeatedly hurting others without making efforts to change. Explanation isn't the same as excuse, and understanding your brain doesn't absolve you of responsibility for your impact on others.

Marriage presents unique challenges and opportunities for ADHD brains. The person you marry will need to understand and adapt to your neurological differences, and you'll need to learn how your ADHD traits affect your spouse and find ways to minimize negative impacts while maximizing positive ones.

Communication about ADHD becomes important in marriage because daily life together will expose all your executive function challenges, emotional patterns, and attention differences. Having ongoing conversations about how these traits affect your relationship and what accommodations or strategies would be helpful can prevent small issues from becoming major conflicts.

Parenting with ADHD brings its own set of relationship dynamics. Your emotional intensity and playfulness might make you a fun, engaging parent, but your time management and organizational challenges might create stress for your children. Learning to use your strengths while building systems to support your weaknesses can help you parent effectively while honoring your neurological design.

If you're parenting ADHD children, understanding your own patterns can help you recognize and support theirs. The emotional dysregulation, attention challenges, and social struggles you've experienced can give you empathy and insight for helping your children navigate similar issues.

Friendships might require different maintenance strategies for ADHD brains. You might need to be more intentional about staying in touch because time blindness makes months feel like weeks. You might need to schedule friend time in your calendar because otherwise it gets lost among more urgent demands. You might need to communicate about your social energy levels because you can't maintain consistent social availability.

> ⚠ **Caution:** Avoid oversharing about your ADHD struggles in new relationships. Build trust gradually before revealing vulnerabilities, and gauge whether people can handle the complexity of your neurological reality.

Some friends will understand and adapt to your ADHD traits. Others might not. Learning to identify which relationships are sustainable given your neurological needs and which ones require too much masking or emotional labor can help you invest your limited social energy wisely.

The church community presents both opportunities and challenges for ADHD relationships. The emphasis on love, acceptance, and community can provide deep belonging for people who have often felt different or misunderstood. Church social dynamics can also trigger RSD, and the expectations for consistency and traditional forms of service might not match your natural patterns.

Finding ways to serve and connect that match your gifts and energy patterns can help you contribute to church community without burning out. This might mean being involved in crisis response instead of ongoing committees, doing hands-on service instead of administrative work, or connecting with people one-on-one instead of in large group settings.

Paul's description of love in 1 Corinthians 13 provides a framework for healthy relationships that acknowledges both the goal and the process. Love is patient—with yourself and others as you learn to navigate relationships with ADHD traits. Love is kind—extending grace when communication doesn't go perfectly. Love is not proud—being willing to acknowledge when your ADHD behaviors have hurt someone and taking steps to repair the relationship.

The goal isn't perfect communication or flawless relationships. The goal is authentic connection with people who understand and accept your neurological differences while still holding you accountable for treating others with love and respect. This requires finding people who can see past your ADHD traits to your heart while also being willing to adapt your communication and relationship styles to serve others well.

> **✗ Danger Zone:** Avoid relationships with people who consistently shame you for ADHD traits you can't control. Healthy relationships accommodate neurological differences without enabling harmful behaviors, but they don't attack you for being neurodivergent.

Your ADHD brain brings unique gifts to relationships: deep empathy, emotional intensity, creative problem-solving, and passionate engagement. Learning to steward these gifts well while managing the challenges that come with them is part of loving others as Christ has loved you.

Part III: Workplace and Calling - Using Your Gifts

ADHD in the Workplace

"Whatever you do, work at it with all your heart, as working for the Lord, not for human masters, since you know that you will receive an inheritance from the Lord as a reward. It is the Lord Christ you are serving." (Colossians 3:23-24, NIV)

"A person's gifts will make room for them and bring them before the great." (Proverbs 18:16, NIV)

"Each of you should use whatever gift you have to serve others, as faithful stewards of God's grace in its various forms." (1 Peter 4:10, NIV)

You sit at your desk staring at the quarterly report that's been due for three days. Your brain feels like it's wrapped in cotton. The spreadsheet numbers blur together, and you can't seem to make progress despite sitting there for two hours. Your coworker in the next cubicle is chatting on the phone, someone's heating fish in the microwave, and the fluorescent lights are humming at a frequency that makes your teeth itch.

Meanwhile, your brain is composing the perfect response to an email you received yesterday, designing a better system for client intake, and wondering if your manager noticed that you were five minutes late this morning because you couldn't find your keys. Everything except the report that's due feels more interesting and urgent.

You check your phone for the fifteenth time, scroll through three news articles, and reorganize your desk supplies. By lunch, you've accomplished everything except the one thing you needed to do. The familiar cocktail of anxiety, shame, and self-loathing begins brewing as you realize you'll probably be staying late again tonight, assuming you can focus any better then than you can now.

You're trying to be productive in a system that wasn't built with your brain in mind. The gap between your actual performance and your potential performance isn't a character issue. It's an engineering mismatch.

The traditional workplace runs on assumptions that have nothing to do with how your brain actually works. Focus on demand. Quiet environments. Consistent output across the day. Systematic task management. When none of these come naturally, it's easy to conclude you're lazy or undisciplined. You're not. You're running the wrong software on the wrong hardware.

★ **Pro Tip:** Document your accommodation needs and successes to build a case for workplace modifications. Keep records of how accommodations improved your productivity or prevented errors. Concrete evidence helps employers understand the business benefits.

Paul's instruction to work "with all your heart, as working for the Lord" doesn't specify what that work should look like or how it should be organized. The principle of wholehearted service remains constant, but the application needs to account for how your ADHD brain engages with work most effectively.

Your natural work rhythms are the most important thing most productivity advice will never tell you about.

Traditional productivity advice is written for brains that respond to willpower. Yours doesn't. Your attention runs on weather patterns, not switches. Some days will be clear and focused. Others will be stormy and scattered. Some projects will naturally capture your hyperfocus. Others will feel like trying to concentrate through a fog.

Learning to work with these patterns instead of fighting them can dramatically improve your workplace effectiveness. This might mean scheduling your most important work during your natural peak focus times, batching similar tasks together to minimize transition costs, or alternating between high-focus and low-focus activities throughout the day.

The open office environment that dominates modern workplaces is challenging for ADHD brains. The constant visual and auditory stimulation can overwhelm your already-scattered attention. Conversations, phone calls, movement, and visual clutter all compete for your brain's processing power, leaving little capacity for focused work.

If you can't control your physical environment, you need strategies to create mental boundaries. Noise-canceling headphones, visual barriers like plants or screens, and designated focus times when you're unavailable for casual interruptions can help create focus islands in a distracting environment.

Time management in the workplace requires different approaches for ADHD brains. Traditional time blocking assumes you can estimate how long tasks will take and stick to predetermined schedules. Your brain might take twenty minutes for a task you thought would take five, or complete in an hour something you expected to take all day.

Flexible time blocking works better than rigid scheduling. Instead of assigning tasks to time slots, block time for types of work: creative tasks, administrative tasks, communication tasks, or deep focus work. This allows you to match your current brain state and energy level to appropriate activities without the stress of falling behind a too-precise schedule.

The Pomodoro Technique adapts well to ADHD workplace challenges. Twenty-five minutes of focused work followed by a five-minute break can help maintain attention without overwhelming your brain's capacity for sustained focus. During the breaks, you can address the mental interruptions that accumulated during the focus period without losing momentum entirely.

Task initiation, one of the most challenging executive functions for ADHD brains, often becomes the biggest workplace obstacle. You might understand exactly what needs to be done but feel unable to start. The task sits there looking impossible, overwhelming, or unbearably boring while your brain seeks any available distraction.

Breaking tasks into smaller, more concrete components can help overcome initiation paralysis. Instead of "work on client presentation," try "open PowerPoint," then "create title slide," then "find three relevant images." Each small step builds momentum toward the larger goal while providing frequent completion dopamine hits.

> ★ **Pro Tip:** Use the "energy audit" approach to work tasks. Identify which activities drain your ADHD brain and which ones energize it, then negotiate to maximize energizing tasks and minimize draining ones where possible.

The "two-minute rule" can prevent small tasks from becoming overwhelming piles. If something takes less than two minutes, do it immediately instead of adding it to your to-do list. This prevents the mental overhead of tracking small tasks and the guilt that comes from letting them accumulate.

Workplace communication requires careful navigation with ADHD traits. Your enthusiasm and creative thinking can bring valuable perspectives to meetings and projects. Your tendency to interrupt, overshare, or go off on tangents can also derail conversations and frustrate colleagues.

Preparing for meetings by writing down key points you want to make can help you contribute meaningfully without dominating discussions. Taking notes during meetings gives your hands something to do and can help maintain focus. Following up important conversations with email summaries ensures that crucial details don't get lost in your working memory challenges.

Email management becomes crucial for ADHD workplace success because email combines several challenging elements: constant interruption potential, executive function demands for organization and prioritization, and time management challenges. Your inbox can quickly become an overwhelming source of anxiety and distraction.

Setting times for checking and responding to email prevents it from fragmenting your attention throughout the day. Using filters and folders to automatically sort incoming messages reduces the decision fatigue of managing your inbox. Responding immediately to emails that require simple yes/no answers prevents them from cluttering your mental space.

Project management with ADHD requires visual systems that make progress and deadlines concrete instead of abstract. Traditional to-do lists often fail because they don't provide enough context or motivation. Kanban boards, project timelines, and progress trackers can make work more engaging and help maintain momentum.

The hyperfocus aspect of ADHD can be a tremendous workplace asset when channeled appropriately. When you find yourself naturally hyperfocusing on work-related activities, protect that time from interruption. These periods of intense concentration often produce your highest-quality work and can compensate for times when focus is more scattered.

> ⚠ **Caution:** Don't disclose your ADHD to employers without researching company culture and legal protections first. Not all workplaces are safe spaces for neurodivergent disclosure, and some managers might use the information against you despite legal protections.

Learning to recognize the early signs of hyperfocus can help you use it effectively. When you notice yourself becoming deeply absorbed in a task, consider adjusting your schedule to maximize this natural state. This might mean skipping lunch, declining meeting invitations, or working later than usual while the focus lasts.

Hyperfocus also has downsides in workplace contexts. You might become so absorbed in perfecting one aspect of a project that you neglect other important deadlines. You might lose track of time and miss meetings or appointments. You might work intensively on interesting tasks while avoiding boring but necessary ones.

Setting external boundaries around hyperfocus can help you channel its benefits while minimizing its costs. Timers, calendar alerts, and accountability partners can help ensure that hyperfocus doesn't derail other responsibilities.

⚠ **Caution:** Avoid taking on extra responsibilities during hyperfocus periods without considering your baseline capacity. What feels manageable during peak performance might overwhelm you when your brain returns to normal functioning.

Workplace relationships require special attention with ADHD traits. Your emotional intensity and empathy can make you a supportive colleague and valuable team member. Your impulsivity and rejection sensitivity can also create interpersonal challenges that affect your professional reputation and career advancement.

Learning to separate work relationships from personal friendships can help maintain appropriate professional boundaries. This doesn't mean being cold or unfriendly. It means being strategic about how much personal information you share and how emotionally involved you become in workplace dynamics.

The rejection sensitivity that affects personal relationships also impacts workplace interactions. Constructive feedback can feel like personal attacks. Not being invited to casual social events can trigger feelings of exclusion. Performance reviews can activate shame spirals even when the feedback is largely positive.

Strategies for managing RSD in professional contexts become crucial for career success. This might mean asking for feedback in writing so you can process it privately before responding, scheduling time to decompress after difficult conversations, or working with a therapist to develop resilience against workplace triggers.

Career choice becomes important for ADHD brains because the match between your neurological patterns and job requirements affects your success and satisfaction. Jobs that require sustained attention to boring tasks, detailed record-keeping, or consistent routine may be poor fits regardless of your effort and dedication.

Look for careers that use your natural strengths: creativity, problem-solving, crisis management, empathy, innovation, or high-stimulation environments. Jobs in emergency services, creative fields, entrepreneurship, counseling, or dynamic team environments might align better with your brain's preferences than traditional office roles.

✕ Danger Zone: Avoid jobs that require sustained attention to boring tasks without any accommodation possibilities. Some work environments are fundamentally incompatible with ADHD brains, and trying to force compatibility often leads to burnout and mental health crises.

The gig economy and remote work options can provide flexibility that accommodates ADHD work patterns. Being able to control your environment, schedule, and task variety can dramatically improve your productivity and job satisfaction. These arrangements also require strong self-management skills that might need development.

Workplace accommodations can level the playing field for ADHD employees. Under the Americans with Disabilities Act, you may be entitled to reasonable accommodations that help you perform your job effectively. These might include flexible scheduling, noise-reducing headphones, written instructions instead of verbal ones, or modified workspace arrangements.

Deciding whether to disclose your ADHD diagnosis to employers requires careful consideration of the workplace culture, your job security, and the potential benefits versus risks. Some employers are supportive and willing to provide accommodations. Others might view ADHD as a liability despite legal protections.

If you choose to disclose, focus on how accommodations will improve your performance instead of on your limitations. Frame the conversation around solutions and productivity instead of problems and deficits. Come prepared with accommodation requests and examples of how they've helped you succeed in the past.

A support network at work can help you navigate ADHD challenges and use your strengths. This might include finding a mentor who understands neurodiversity, connecting with other employees who have ADHD, or working with HR to create more inclusive workplace policies.

Proverbs 18:16 reminds us that our gifts will make room for us. Your ADHD brain brings unique abilities to the workplace: creativity, innovation, empathy, crisis management skills, and fresh perspectives on old problems. The challenge is finding work environments and roles that value these gifts while providing support for the areas where you struggle.

Working "with all your heart" as Paul instructs doesn't mean working in ways that exhaust and frustrate you. It means finding ways to channel your passion, creativity, and unique perspectives into meaningful work that serves others and honors God. This might require advocating for yourself, seeking accommodations, or even changing careers to find better alignment between your calling and your neurological design.

Your ADHD brain isn't a workplace liability that needs to be overcome. It's a different type of professional asset that needs to be understood, supported, and channeled effectively. When you find the right match between your gifts and your work environment, your supposed weaknesses can become your greatest professional strengths.

Workplace success for ADHD brains often looks different from neurotypical career paths. Your path might involve more job changes, career pivots, or unconventional arrangements. This isn't failure or instability. It's the process of finding work that truly matches how God designed your brain to contribute to His kingdom and serve others in the world.

Creativity and Innovation

"Then the Lord said to Moses, 'See, I have chosen Bezalel son of Uri, the son of Hur, of the tribe of Judah, and I have filled him with the Spirit of God, with wisdom, with understanding, with knowledge and with all kinds of skills—to make artistic designs for work in gold, silver and bronze, to cut and set stones, to work in wood, and to engage in all kinds of crafts.'"
(Exodus 31:2-5, NIV)

"He has made everything beautiful in its time. He has also set eternity in the human heart; yet no one can fathom what God has done from beginning to end." (Ecclesiastes 3:11, NIV)

You're sitting in yet another brainstorming meeting where everyone is supposed to think outside the box. The facilitator writes the problem on the whiteboard and asks for creative solutions. Your neurotypical colleagues offer predictable suggestions: incremental improvements to existing processes, minor variations on what's already been tried, safe ideas that won't ruffle any feathers.

Meanwhile, your brain is exploding with connections. You see seventeen different ways to approach the problem, three of which involve completely reframing the question itself. You're making connections between this challenge and something you read about bee colonies, a conversation you had with your barber last week, and a documentary about jazz improvisation. Your ideas feel so obvious to you that you assume everyone else is seeing the same possibilities.

> ★ **Pro Tip:** Keep a "random ideas" notebook (physical or digital) to capture creative thoughts before they disappear into the ADHD void. Your best ideas often come at inconvenient times when you can't act on them immediately, but you can preserve them for later development.

When you finally share one of your ideas, the room goes quiet. Someone says, "That's... interesting." Another person asks how much it would cost, as if innovation should come with a price tag attached. The facilitator writes your idea on the board with obvious reluctance and quickly moves on to safer territory.

You leave the meeting frustrated, wondering why organizations say they want creativity but seem uncomfortable when they encounter it. What you don't realize is that your ADHD brain just demonstrated one of its greatest superpowers: the ability to see patterns, make unexpected connections, and generate truly novel solutions to complex problems.

The same neural differences that make it hard to focus on boring tasks also enable breakthrough thinking that neurotypical minds struggle to access. Your distractibility isn't just a limitation. It's also a feature that allows you to notice things others miss and make connections across seemingly unrelated domains.

⚠ **Caution:** Avoid creative perfectionism that prevents you from sharing or completing projects. Your ADHD brain generates more ideas than you can perfect, so focus on completion and iteration instead of flawless execution.

When God called Bezalel to design and create the tabernacle, He didn't choose someone with conventional artistic training or predictable design sensibilities. He chose someone and filled him with divine creativity to envision something entirely new. The tabernacle wasn't an incremental improvement on existing religious architecture. It was a revolutionary design that combined beauty, functionality, and spiritual symbolism in ways that had never been attempted before.

Your ADHD brain operates with similar creative freedom when it's engaged with problems that capture your interest. The same scattered attention that makes mundane tasks difficult enables you to hold multiple perspectives simultaneously, switch rapidly between different approaches, and synthesize information from diverse sources into novel solutions.

> ★ **Pro Tip:** Schedule dedicated "creative chaos" time where you can hyperfocus on innovative projects without guilt about neglecting other responsibilities. Protect this time as fiercely as you would any other important commitment.

Divergent thinking is one of ADHD's core strengths. Where neurotypical brains converge on the single best answer, yours keeps generating more questions and more possibilities. It naturally explores multiple angles, questions assumptions, and approaches challenges from unexpected angles.

This divergent thinking shows up in how you process information. When neurotypical people read about a business problem, they might think linearly about business solutions. Your brain might connect that problem to principles from nature, insights from history, patterns from psychology, or analogies from completely unrelated fields. These cross-domain connections often lead to breakthrough innovations that more focused thinking would never discover.

The problem is that most organizations say they want creativity and mean they want slightly better versions of what they already have. Schools teach students to find the right answer, not to generate better questions. Businesses value predictable processes over creative experimentation. Churches often prefer familiar traditions over anything that might make the 10:30 service run long.

> ✗ **Danger Zone:** Don't let others discourage your creative explorations just because they seem impractical or scattered. Many innovations came from ADHD-style thinking that others initially dismissed as unrealistic or unfocused.

Innovation requires exactly the kind of thinking your brain does when nobody's forcing it to sit still. Revolutionary advances come from people who can see beyond current limitations, who notice patterns that others miss, who ask questions that challenge fundamental assumptions. Your scattered attention might be exactly what's needed to solve problems that conventional thinking has failed to address.

The hyperfocus aspect of ADHD can become a powerful innovation tool when directed toward creative challenges. When something captures your intense interest, you can dive deeper than most people have the patience or attention span to go. You notice subtleties and nuances that escape casual observation. You persist through obstacles that would discourage more conventional thinkers.

Some of history's greatest innovations have come from people whose minds worked differently from the norm. Thomas Edison's restless energy and constant experimentation reflect patterns we now recognize as ADHD-like. Steve Jobs's ability to envision products that didn't yet exist and his impatience with incremental improvements suggest neurodivergent thinking. Many artists, inventors, and entrepreneurs display the kind of creative intensity and unconventional approaches that characterize ADHD brains.

Your brain's need for stimulation can drive innovation when channeled productively. Boredom with existing solutions motivates you to find better approaches. Frustration with inefficient systems pushes you to design improvements. Impatience with slow progress drives you to find faster methods. The same restlessness that makes you difficult to manage in traditional environments can become fuel for creative breakthrough.

The emotional intensity that comes with ADHD can also fuel creative innovation. Your passion for causes you care about can drive you to find solutions that others wouldn't invest the emotional energy to pursue. Your empathy for people who are struggling can motivate you to design products, services, or systems that address real human needs. Your frustration with injustice can inspire you to create new approaches to social problems.

Creativity requires more than just generating ideas. It requires the ability to develop, refine, and implement those ideas effectively. This is where many ADHD innovators struggle. The same brain that excels at generating possibilities often struggles with the sustained focus and detailed execution required to bring ideas to fruition.

This pattern, once you see it, can help you structure your creative work more effectively. Partner with people who excel at implementation and project management. Focus your energy on the ideation and early development phases where your strengths are most valuable. Build teams that complement your abilities instead of trying to handle every aspect of innovation yourself.

The iterative nature of innovation aligns well with ADHD thinking patterns. Your brain naturally wants to try multiple approaches, experiment with variations, and test different possibilities. Instead of seeing this as lack of focus, recognize it as a natural innovation methodology. Rapid prototyping, design thinking, and agile development approaches were essentially designed for minds that work like yours.

★ **Pro Tip:** Use the "idea parking lot" technique during structured activities. Write down creative thoughts that arise during meetings or focused work, then return to them during designated creative time. This honors both your innovative brain and your current responsibilities.

Your ability to shift perspectives quickly can be invaluable for innovation. When one approach isn't working, you can pivot to completely different strategies without the sunk-cost thinking that traps more linear minds. When you encounter obstacles, you can reframe problems in ways that reveal new solution pathways. This cognitive flexibility is essential for breakthrough innovation.

The tendency to question authority and challenge conventional wisdom is genuinely disruptive in environments that reward compliance. It's genuinely valuable in environments that need someone to say the obvious thing nobody else will say. Most of the significant changes in churches, organizations, and communities start with someone who couldn't stop asking why. That's often you.

Innovation also requires the ability to build on existing knowledge instead of starting from scratch every time. Your brain's preference for novelty might lead you to dismiss valuable conventional approaches in favor of untested alternatives. Learning to appreciate both tradition and innovation, both proven methods and experimental approaches, can make your creativity more effective.

The church needs innovative thinking to address rapidly changing cultural contexts and emerging social challenges. Traditional approaches to evangelism, discipleship, and community engagement may not connect with younger generations or diverse cultural groups. Your ADHD brain's ability to see fresh possibilities and design new approaches can help the church adapt without compromising core biblical principles.

Innovation in ministry might involve creating new worship formats that engage different learning styles and attention spans. It might mean developing discipleship programs that work for neurodivergent minds. It might involve using technology in creative ways to build community and support spiritual growth. Your ability to think beyond conventional church models can help reach people who haven't been effectively served by traditional approaches.

Entrepreneurship can be a natural fit for ADHD brains because it rewards innovation, tolerates risk-taking, and allows you to create work environments that match your neurological needs. Many successful entrepreneurs display ADHD traits: high energy, creative problem-solving, willingness to challenge conventional wisdom, and ability to see opportunities that others miss.

Entrepreneurship also requires sustained execution, which can be challenging for ADHD minds. The same creative restlessness that generates business ideas can make it difficult to focus on the detailed work required to build successful companies.

Surrounding yourself with partners and team members who complement your strengths becomes essential for entrepreneurial success.

The rapid pace of technological change creates increasing demand for the kind of innovative thinking that ADHD brains provide naturally. Artificial intelligence, automation, and digital transformation are disrupting traditional industries and creating needs for creative solutions. Your ability to adapt quickly, think flexibly, and generate novel approaches becomes increasingly valuable in this environment.

Creative fields like design, advertising, entertainment, and media often appreciate the fresh perspectives and unconventional approaches that ADHD minds bring. Your ability to see things differently, make unexpected connections, and generate original ideas can be significant professional assets in these industries.

Creativity isn't limited to traditionally creative fields. Every industry needs innovation. Healthcare needs better patient care systems. Education needs more effective teaching methods. Finance needs more accessible services. Manufacturing needs more efficient processes. Your ADHD brain's innovative capabilities can contribute to progress in any field that interests you.

The key is learning to channel your creative energy strategically instead of scattering it across too many projects simultaneously. Your brain naturally generates more ideas than you can possibly pursue. Criteria for evaluating and prioritizing creative opportunities can help you focus your limited time and energy on the most promising possibilities.

Ecclesiastes 3:11 reminds us that God "has made everything beautiful in its time" and "has set eternity in the human heart." Your ADHD brain's drive toward innovation and creativity reflects something of God's own creative nature. The same divine spark that inspired Bezalel to design the tabernacle continues to inspire believers to create beautiful, useful, and meaningful innovations that serve others and honor God.

Your creative gifts aren't accidents or side effects of your neurological differences. They're central to how God designed you to contribute to His kingdom and serve the world. The church, the workplace, and society all need the fresh perspectives, innovative solutions, and creative energy that your ADHD brain naturally provides.

Learning to steward your creativity well means understanding both its power and its limitations. It means building teams and systems that support your innovative thinking while compensating for areas where you struggle. It means choosing projects and environments that engage your creative passion while providing enough structure to ensure productive outcomes.

The world needs what your ADHD brain has to offer. The same traits that made you feel different or difficult in traditional educational and workplace settings may be exactly what's needed to solve problems that conventional thinking has failed to address. Your creativity isn't a consolation prize for dealing with ADHD challenges. It's one of your greatest gifts to offer a world that desperately needs fresh thinking and innovative solutions.

"Now to each one the manifestation of the Spirit is given for the common good. To one there is given through the Spirit a message of wisdom, to another a message of knowledge by means of the same Spirit, to another faith by the same Spirit, to another gifts of healing by the same Spirit, to another miraculous powers, to another prophecy, to another distinguishing between spirits, to another speaking in different kinds of tongues, and to still another the interpretation of tongues. All these are the work of one and the same Spirit, and he distributes them to each one, just as he determines." (1 Corinthians 12:7-11, NIV)

"But he said to me, 'My grace is sufficient for you, for my power is made perfect in weakness.' Therefore I will boast all the more gladly about my weaknesses, so that Christ's power may rest on me." (2 Corinthians 12:9, NIV)

"As each part does its work, the whole body grows and builds itself up in love." (Ephesians 4:16, NIV)

You volunteered to help with the church's community outreach program because you felt passionate about serving the homeless population in your city. The organizing committee scheduled weekly planning meetings every Tuesday at 7 PM to coordinate volunteers, plan meals, and discuss logistics. You showed up enthusiastically for the first three meetings, taking detailed notes and offering creative ideas for improving the program.

By the fourth meeting, you're struggling to stay engaged as the discussion drags through the same agenda items week after week. Your mind wanders during the budget review. You zone out during the volunteer scheduling discussion. When someone mentions that Mrs. Henderson always brings too much potato salad, you impulsively suggest just asking her to bring something else, only to discover there's apparently a complex history involving Mrs. Henderson's feelings about her potato salad that requires delicate navigation.

My introduction to organized religion came with a front-row seat to its worst possibilities. The church I grew up in took enormous pride in doing everything by the book — chapter and verse for every doctrine, no instruments during worship because the Bible didn't specifically mention them, careful adherence to scriptural patterns at every turn. The precision was impressive.

What disappeared completely when it actually mattered was something else. The same people who could debate whether communion bread should be leavened or unleavened missed obvious commandments entirely when following them would have cost them something. Ritual precision and moral courage, it turned out, had nothing to do with each other.

I tell you this not to poison your view of the church but because if you're an ADHD Christian with a complicated relationship with religious institutions, your skepticism probably has a foundation in real experience. You've likely seen the gap between what gets preached and what gets practiced. You've probably been on the receiving end of spiritual language used to shame rather than heal.

That experience doesn't disqualify you from ministry. In some ways it equips you for it. People who have been failed by institutions are often best positioned to build something better — more honest, more accessible, less interested in performance and more interested in the actual humans in the room. Your ADHD brain's radar for inauthenticity is a feature in that work, not a liability.

I know what it's like to find the right church and then lose it — not by leaving, but by watching it change into something you didn't sign up for.

The pastor who drew me in preached about how Christ makes you better, why belief matters, how faith actually helps people navigate real life. That's what got me through the door and kept me coming back through a year of waiting to be baptized. His sermons had a people focus. They were about something.

Then he handed the church to his son.

The shift was jarring. The new sermons were about damnation, about donation, about how giving money was the path to Christ's good grace. One week there was a fundraising pitch for a decorative light wall. I sat there thinking about the year I'd spent white-knuckling my way to baptism in that building, and I couldn't reconcile the two things.

For ADHD Christians, this kind of institutional change hits differently than it might for someone with a longer runway of church experience to draw on. When you've spent significant willpower getting through the door, when the church finally worked because of specific things a specific person was doing, losing those things isn't just disappointing. It can feel like the evidence you always suspected was out there — that this was never really going to hold.

I'm looking for another church. That sentence is harder to write than it should be, because it means starting over: rebuilding trust, re-exposing myself to environments that have historically been painful, burning more of the willpower I spent a year depleting just to get baptized in the first place.

If you've been here — if you found something that worked and then watched it stop working through no fault of your own — your exhaustion is legitimate. So is the looking. The fact that you're still looking is not a small thing. It's actually the whole point.

★ **Pro Tip:** Volunteer for short-term projects before committing to ongoing ministry roles. Test your capacity and interest level with defined endpoints instead of open-ended commitments that might overwhelm your executive function.

By week six, you're dreading the meetings but forcing yourself to attend because you committed to the program. By week eight, you've stopped coming to meetings altogether, feeling guilty and ashamed that you can't sustain interest in something you genuinely care about. Eventually, you drift away from the outreach program entirely, chalking up another ministry failure to your apparent inability to stick with anything long-term.

Your ADHD brain is wired for certain types of ministry. Just not the types most churches organize around. Creative problem-solving, crisis response, emotional empathy, passionate engagement — those are real assets for kingdom work. The problem is that most church structures were built around weekly meetings and long-term committees, which is approximately the worst possible format for how your brain operates.

The problem isn't that you're not called to serve. The problem is that traditional church ministry structures were designed by and for neurotypical brains that thrive on routine, systematic organization, and long-term commitments to predictable activities. Your brain operates differently, and it needs different types of service opportunities to flourish.

> ⚠ **Caution:** Don't say yes to ministry opportunities just because no one else volunteers. Burnout serves no one, and taking on roles that drain you prevents you from using your real gifts effectively.

Paul's description of spiritual gifts in 1 Corinthians 12 emphasizes that the Spirit distributes different gifts to different people "just as he determines." This distribution isn't random or accidental. God intentionally creates diversity in the body of Christ because different types of people are needed for different types of kingdom work.

Your ADHD brain brings unique capabilities to ministry that neurotypical minds often struggle with. Your ability to think on your feet makes you excellent in crisis situations where quick decisions and adaptive responses are needed. Your emotional intensity enables deep empathy with people who are hurting. Your creativity helps you find innovative solutions to ministry challenges. Your passion, when engaged, can inspire and motivate others.

> ★ **Pro Tip:** Partner with detail-oriented people in ministry roles. Your big-picture thinking and creative problem-solving can complement someone else's organizational skills and attention to logistics. Teams use everyone's strengths.

The key is finding ministry opportunities that match your neurological strengths instead of forcing yourself into roles that require your areas of weakness. This might mean focusing on short-term, project-based service instead of ongoing committee work. It might mean serving in crisis response roles instead of administrative positions. It might mean working directly with people instead of managing programs.

Crisis ministry can be an ideal fit for ADHD brains. When natural disasters strike, when families face emergencies, when people need immediate practical help, your ability to mobilize quickly and think creatively under pressure becomes invaluable. The urgency and variety of crisis situations provide the stimulation your brain needs to engage fully.

Your hyperfocus can become a powerful ministry tool when directed toward people and causes you care about deeply. When someone you're counseling or mentoring captures your passionate interest, you can provide levels of attention and support that help support real transformation. Your ability to dive deep into understanding their situation and brainstorming solutions can be life-changing for the people you serve.

Hyperfocus in ministry also requires wisdom and boundaries. You might become so absorbed in helping one person that you neglect other responsibilities or relationships. You might take on more emotional weight than you can healthily carry. Learning to recognize when your ministry hyperfocus is becoming unhealthy and building systems to maintain balance becomes crucial.

Your emotional intensity can enable profound compassion and connection with people who are struggling. You feel others' pain deeply, which motivates you to provide practical help and emotional support. Your own experiences with rejection, failure, and feeling different can give you authentic empathy for people facing similar challenges.

This emotional engagement can also become overwhelming if not managed carefully. Your brain might absorb so much of others' emotional pain that you become depleted and burned out. Learning to set emotional boundaries while still maintaining genuine compassion is an essential skill for sustainable ministry.

The ADHD tendency to challenge conventional approaches can bring fresh perspectives to ministry challenges. You might question why things are done certain ways and propose innovative alternatives. Your impatience with ineffective systems can motivate improvements that better serve people's needs. Your outside-the-box thinking can help churches reach people who haven't been effectively engaged by traditional approaches.

Challenging conventional wisdom in church contexts requires wisdom and tact. Your direct communication style and impatience with bureaucracy might come across as disrespectful or rebellious even when your motivations are pure. Learning to frame innovative suggestions diplomatically and work within existing structures while advocating for change becomes important for effective ministry leadership.

Teaching and preaching can be natural fits for ADHD brains when the content genuinely engages your passion. Your enthusiasm can be contagious, helping others connect with biblical truths in fresh ways. Your creative thinking can help you illustrate complex concepts through stories, analogies, and real-world applications that resonate with diverse audiences.

Your tendency toward tangential thinking might also lead to scattered presentations that lose focus and confuse listeners. Your impulsivity might cause you to say things without fully considering how they'll be received. Learning to structure your teaching carefully while still allowing room for spontaneous insights can help you communicate effectively.

Pastoral care can be an area where ADHD traits become significant strengths. Your ability to read emotional cues and respond with immediate compassion can provide comfort and support to people in crisis. Your creative problem-solving can help you find practical solutions to complex personal problems. Your passion for helping others can motivate you to go above and beyond in providing care.

The unstructured nature of pastoral care might also present challenges for your executive function. You might struggle to follow up consistently, forget important details about people's situations, or have difficulty maintaining professional boundaries. Building systems to track pastoral interactions and setting clear limits on your availability can help you provide care sustainably.

> ★ **Pro Tip:** Use "time boxing" for overwhelming tasks. Set a timer for 15-25 minutes and work on organization or financial tasks only until the timer goes off. This prevents executive function paralysis while making progress.

Youth ministry often appeals to ADHD brains because it requires high energy, creativity, and the ability to connect with young people who may themselves be dealing with attention and behavioral challenges. Your playfulness and unconventional thinking can help you design engaging activities and connect with kids who don't fit traditional molds.

Working with youth also requires consistency and reliable leadership, which can be challenging for ADHD brains. Young people need adults they can count on to show up and follow through on commitments. Building accountability systems and partnering with more detail-oriented volunteers can help ensure that your creative energy is supported by reliable structure.

Music ministry can provide an outlet for the creative and emotional intensity that characterizes many ADHD brains. Whether leading worship, playing instruments, or organizing special music events, this type of ministry can engage your artistic gifts while serving the church community.

The performance aspects of music ministry might also trigger anxiety or perfectionism for people with rejection sensitivity. The visible nature of musical mistakes and the subjective nature of artistic preferences can activate RSD in ways that make this ministry challenging despite natural musical gifts.

Missions work, both short-term and long-term, can appeal to ADHD brains because it involves adventure, cultural variety, and often requires the kind of adaptability and creative problem-solving that you naturally provide. The intensity and significance of missions work can engage your passion in ways that sustain focus and motivation.

The practical challenges of living and working in unfamiliar environments might also amplify executive function difficulties. Managing logistics, navigating cultural differences, and maintaining personal organization in challenging conditions can be overwhelming for ADHD brains that already struggle with these areas.

Social justice ministry can be a natural fit for the passion and moral intensity that many ADHD Christians feel. Your ability to see systemic problems and envision innovative solutions can contribute to advocacy work, community organizing, and direct service to marginalized populations.

The long-term nature of social change work might conflict with your brain's preference for immediate results and novel challenges. Learning to find satisfaction in incremental progress and building sustainable rhythms for justice work can help you contribute effectively without burning out.

Administrative roles in church leadership often present the greatest challenges for ADHD brains. Board meetings, budget planning, policy development, and organizational management require exactly the types of sustained attention to detail that ADHD brains struggle with most. If you find yourself in administrative roles, focus on delegating detail work while contributing your strengths in vision-casting, creative problem-solving, and people leadership.

> ⚠ **Caution:** Avoid ministry roles that require skills you're still developing in your personal life. If you struggle with organization at home, don't volunteer to organize the church's storage closet until you've built those skills in lower-stakes environments.

Paul's statement that God's power is made perfect in weakness takes on special meaning for ADHD Christians in ministry. Your neurological differences create both limitations and unique capabilities. The same traits that make certain types of ministry challenging also create opportunities for serving in ways that neurotypical minds might not be equipped for.

A sustainable ministry life requires understanding both your gifts and your limitations. This might mean saying no to ministry opportunities that don't match your strengths, even when they seem important or when you feel pressured to volunteer. It might mean asking for accommodations or support that help you serve effectively in roles that engage your passions.

Partnering with people whose gifts complement yours can create ministry teams that accomplish more than either of you could individually. Your creative vision paired with someone else's detailed execution can produce powerful results. Your passionate advocacy supported by someone else's diplomatic skills can create lasting change.

> ✘ **Danger Zone:** Avoid ministry roles that primarily require skills in your areas of greatest challenge. Playing to your strengths serves the kingdom better than martyring yourself in your weaknesses while disappointing everyone involved.

The goal isn't to overcome your ADHD traits so you can serve like neurotypical Christians. The goal is to understand how God wants to use your unique wiring for His purposes. The church needs the creativity, passion, empathy, and innovative thinking that ADHD brains bring. Finding the right fit between your gifts and ministry opportunities allows you to serve with joy and effectiveness.

Your ADHD brain wasn't a mistake in God's design for your life and ministry. It's a tool He's given you for certain types of kingdom work. When you find ministry roles that match your neurological design, your supposed weaknesses become strengths that serve others and glorify God in ways that conventional approaches never could.

The body of Christ is designed to include all kinds of minds, personalities, and gifts. Your role isn't to become someone else so you can serve better. Your role is to become more fully yourself so you can serve in the unique ways God designed you to contribute to His kingdom work in the world.

Part IV: Special Challenges

Addictive Behaviors and Impulse Control

"All things are lawful for me,' but not all things are helpful. 'All things are lawful for me,' but I will not be dominated by anything." (1 Corinthians 6:12, NIV)

"But the fruit of the Spirit is love, joy, peace, forbearance, kindness, goodness, faithfulness, gentleness and self-control. Against such things there is no law." (Galatians 5:22-23, NIV)

It starts innocently enough. You're feeling understimulated and bored, so you pick up your phone to check social media for "just a minute." Three hours later, you're still scrolling through endless feeds, your brain caught in a dopamine loop that you can't seem to break. You've missed dinner, ignored your family, and accomplished none of the things you intended to do tonight. The familiar mixture of shame and self-loathing washes over you as you realize you've done it again.

Or maybe it's shopping. You're having a rough day, feeling rejected and inadequate, so you decide to browse online stores to cheer yourself up. One purchase leads to another, and before you know it, you've spent money you don't have on things you don't need. The temporary high of buying something new quickly fades, replaced by anxiety about your credit card balance and guilt about your lack of self-control.

Perhaps it's food, Netflix binges, video games, or something more serious like alcohol or drugs. The substance or behavior varies, but the underlying pattern remains the same: your ADHD brain seeks stimulation and relief from uncomfortable emotions, finds temporary satisfaction in addictive behaviors, then crashes into shame and regret when the high wears off.

> **✗ Danger Zone:** Avoid shame-based accountability that focuses on failure instead of recovery and growth. Shame fuels addictive cycles instead of breaking them, and judgment from others often drives behavior underground instead of healing it.

Your brain's neurochemical differences make you more vulnerable to addictive behaviors while simultaneously making it harder to develop the self-control necessary to break free from them. This isn't a character flaw or spiritual weakness. It's a predictable consequence of how ADHD brains function in a world full of highly stimulating, instantly gratifying options.

ADHD brains have lower baseline levels of dopamine, the neurotransmitter associated with pleasure, motivation, and reward. This means you constantly feel slightly understimulated and seek activities that will provide the dopamine hits your brain craves. Unfortunately, many of the most readily available dopamine sources in modern life are also potentially addictive: social media, shopping, gaming, food, substances, and various forms of instant gratification.

Your impulse control system is also compromised by ADHD. The prefrontal cortex, which governs executive functions including impulse control, doesn't function as reliably in ADHD brains. This means the gap between wanting something and acting on that want is shorter and less filtered than in neurotypical brains. You feel an urge, and before your rational mind can evaluate whether acting on it is wise, you've already reached for your phone, opened the shopping app, or grabbed the snack.

> **★ Pro Tip:** Replace dopamine-seeking behaviors with healthier alternatives before trying to eliminate them entirely. Your brain needs stimulation, so provide it through exercise, creative projects, or social connection instead of leaving a void that demands filling.

Paul's words in 1 Corinthians 6:12 take on special significance for ADHD Christians: "All things are lawful for me, but I will not be dominated by anything." The challenge isn't just avoiding obviously sinful behaviors. It's recognizing when seemingly innocent activities have gained dominion over your thoughts, time, and energy. Your brain's need for stimulation can turn almost anything into a compulsive behavior if you're not careful.

The shame cycle that accompanies addictive behaviors is brutal for ADHD brains. You engage in the behavior, feel guilty about your lack of self-control, use that guilt as evidence that you're a failure, then seek comfort in the very behavior that caused the guilt in the first place. Each cycle reinforces both the addiction and the shame, creating a downward spiral that feels impossible to escape.

This shame is often compounded by spiritual guilt. You know that self-control is a fruit of the Spirit. You believe that Christ has set you free from slavery to sin. You want to honor God with your choices. But your brain keeps betraying your best intentions, leaving you feeling like a spiritual failure who can't access the power that's supposedly available to all believers.

Knowing the neurological basis of addictive behaviors doesn't excuse them, but it does help remove the moral judgment that often makes recovery more difficult. You're not weak, undisciplined, or spiritually immature. You're dealing with a brain that processes rewards and impulses differently than the neurotypical standard, and you need strategies that account for these differences.

Screen addiction has become one of the most common struggles for ADHD brains in the digital age. Social media platforms, video games, streaming services, and even news websites are designed to capture and hold attention through variable reward schedules that trigger dopamine releases. Your brain, already seeking stimulation, becomes easily trapped in these digital dopamine loops.

The infinite scroll design of social media feeds is problematic for ADHD brains. There's always one more post, one more video, one more story to check. Your brain's difficulty with stopping tasks once they're started means you can lose hours to mindless scrolling without realizing how much time has passed. The constant stream of notifications provides regular dopamine hits that reinforce the behavior.

Breaking free from screen addiction requires more than willpower. You need environmental changes that make the addictive behavior harder to access and healthier alternatives easier to choose. This might mean removing apps from your phone, using website blockers during certain hours, or keeping devices out of your bedroom. The goal is to increase friction around the addictive behavior while decreasing friction around positive alternatives.

Shopping addiction appeals to ADHD brains because it provides immediate gratification, novelty, and a temporary escape from negative emotions. The excitement of finding something new and the anticipation of how it will improve your life can create powerful dopamine hits. Online shopping is dangerous because it eliminates the natural delays and social accountability that might interrupt impulsive purchases.

Retail therapy often serves as emotional regulation for ADHD brains. When you're feeling rejected, inadequate, or overwhelmed, buying something new can provide temporary relief from those uncomfortable emotions. The problem is that this relief is short-lived, and the underlying emotional issues remain unaddressed while new problems (debt, clutter, guilt) are added to the mix.

Impulse control around spending requires practical strategies that work with your brain's limitations instead of relying on willpower alone. The 24-hour rule, where you wait a full day before making non-essential purchases, gives your prefrontal cortex time to engage and evaluate whether you really need the item. Creating wish lists instead of immediately buying things allows you to experience some of the satisfaction of "getting" something without the financial consequences.

★ **Pro Tip:** Use the "pause and pray" technique for impulse control. When you feel the urge to engage in problematic behavior, commit to praying for 60 seconds first. This brief delay often allows prefrontal cortex function to catch up with impulse.

Food addiction and emotional eating are common among ADHD people because food provides both sensory stimulation and emotional comfort. Your brain's seeking system drives you toward highly palatable foods that provide immediate pleasure and distraction from stress or boredom. The same impulsivity that affects other areas of your life can lead to mindless eating or binge episodes.

The diet industry's focus on restriction and willpower sets ADHD brains up for failure. Your brain rebels against rigid rules and responds to deprivation by obsessing about forbidden foods. Instead of relying on self-control, you need strategies that work with your brain's need for variety, stimulation, and immediate satisfaction while still supporting your health goals.

Substance abuse risks are higher for ADHD people, both because of the neurochemical vulnerabilities and because many people use alcohol or drugs to self-medicate ADHD symptoms. Alcohol might seem to quiet mental chatter and reduce social anxiety. Stimulants might help with focus and productivity. Cannabis might help with sleep or emotional regulation. But these temporary benefits come with significant long-term costs.

The Christian community's approach to substance abuse often emphasizes moral choices and spiritual transformation while overlooking the neurobiological factors that make addiction more likely for certain brain types. While spiritual resources are important, they need to be combined with practical strategies that address the underlying neurochemical imbalances and impulse control challenges.

Sexual addiction and pornography use present challenges for ADHD Christians because these behaviors often involve secrecy and shame that conflict directly with Christian values around sexuality. Your brain's need for novelty and intense stimulation can make pornography addictive, while the shame associated with these behaviors can prevent you from seeking help or accountability.

> ⚠ **Caution:** Avoid "white-knuckling" through addictive urges without addressing the underlying need for stimulation. Your ADHD brain will find ways to get dopamine, so provide healthy options instead of hoping the craving disappears.

Breaking free from sexual addiction requires addressing both the neurochemical aspects (finding healthier sources of dopamine and stimulation) and the spiritual aspects (understanding grace, developing accountability, addressing underlying emotional needs). This often requires professional help from counselors who understand both ADHD and Christian sexuality.

Gaming addiction appeals to ADHD brains because games provide constant stimulation, clear feedback systems, and progressive challenges that maintain engagement. The immersive nature of gaming can trigger hyperfocus states that make it difficult to stop playing. Before you know it, hours have passed and important responsibilities have been neglected.

The social aspects of online gaming can also provide connection and achievement that might be lacking in other areas of life. If you struggle with social skills or career success, gaming environments might offer experiences of competence and belonging that feel harder to access in the real world. Understanding these underlying needs is important for developing healthier alternatives.

Workaholism might not seem like an addiction, but for ADHD brains, work can become a compulsive behavior that provides structure, stimulation, and validation while avoiding less comfortable activities like rest, intimacy, or addressing personal problems. Your hyperfocus can make you incredibly productive, but it can also prevent you from maintaining healthy boundaries around work and rest.

The Protestant work ethic and cultural messages about productivity can make workaholism seem virtuous instead of problematic. But Romans 6:12 warns against letting anything, even seemingly good things, reign over your mortal body. When work becomes compulsive instead of intentional, it has crossed the line from stewardship into domination.

Healthy impulse control requires understanding that willpower is a limited resource that gets depleted throughout the day. Instead of relying on self-control, you need systems and environments that make good choices easier and bad choices harder. This might involve meal planning to avoid impulsive food decisions, automatic savings transfers to prevent impulsive spending, or accountability partners who check in on vulnerable areas.

> ★ **Pro Tip:** Create "friction" for impulsive behaviors and remove barriers for healthy ones. Delete shopping apps but keep meditation apps on your home screen. Make destructive choices harder and constructive choices easier.

The concept of "surfing the urge" can be helpful for managing addictive impulses. Instead of trying to fight or ignore cravings, you can observe them with curiosity and compassion, recognizing that they will naturally rise and fall like waves if you don't act on them. This mindfulness approach works better than willpower-based resistance for many ADHD brains.

Recovery from addictive behaviors often requires addressing the underlying needs that the addiction was meeting. If social media was providing connection, you need healthier ways to build relationships. If shopping was providing emotional regulation, you need better stress management tools. If gaming was providing achievement, you need meaningful goals and progress markers in other areas of life.

Professional help is often necessary for breaking free from serious addictive behaviors. Therapists who understand both ADHD and addiction can help you develop personalized strategies that account for your neurological differences.

Support groups can provide community and accountability. In some cases, medication might help address the underlying dopamine imbalances that contribute to addictive behaviors.

> ⚠ **Caution:** Don't assume willpower alone will overcome ADHD-related impulse control issues. Your impulse control is neurologically compromised, not morally deficient, and you need external systems and professional support, not just spiritual disciplines.

Spiritual disciplines can support recovery when adapted for ADHD brains. Prayer, meditation, and Scripture study can provide alternative sources of peace and meaning, but they need to be practiced in ways that work with your attention patterns instead of against them. Short, frequent spiritual practices might be more sustainable than lengthy sessions that require sustained focus.

Grace becomes essential for recovery from addictive behaviors. Shame and guilt often fuel the very behaviors you're trying to overcome. Knowing that your struggles don't disqualify you from God's love and that recovery is a process instead of a single decision can help break the shame cycles that keep you trapped.

The goal isn't perfect self-control but increasing freedom and intentionality in your choices. Some days you'll handle impulses better than others. Some seasons will be easier than others. The measure of progress isn't perfection but the overall trajectory of your life toward health, purpose, and authentic relationship with God and others.

Paul's declaration that he will not be dominated by anything provides both a goal and a grace-filled framework for addressing addictive behaviors. The goal is freedom: not being controlled by substances, behaviors, or compulsions that prevent you from living the life God has called you to live. The grace is in recognizing that this freedom is a gift instead of an achievement, available through Christ's power instead of your own willpower.

Your ADHD brain's vulnerabilities to addictive behaviors are real and need to be taken seriously. But they don't define you or limit what God can do in your life. With the right strategies, support, and spiritual resources, you can develop the freedom and self-control necessary to live with intentionality and purpose, using your unique gifts to serve God and others instead of being dominated by compulsive behaviors that diminish your effectiveness and joy.

Rejection, Failure, and Shame

By the time I was twelve, I had developed a working theory about adults: they lie when it's easier than dealing with problems. They choose what they want to believe over what actually happened, especially if the truth makes their lives more complicated.

It wasn't cynicism. It was empirical. I'd watched teachers let kids get humiliated in front of the class and call it a lesson. I'd seen institutions close ranks around their own reputation rather than protect the people they claimed to serve. I'd been told repeatedly that what I clearly saw with my own eyes wasn't what happened.

So I stopped expecting the official version of anything to match reality, and I started paying attention to what people actually did rather than what they said they were doing.

For ADHD Christians, shame often gets layered on top of exactly this kind of accumulated experience. You're not just dealing with the shame of forgetting things or losing focus. You're often dealing with decades of having your perception corrected, your reality reframed, your genuine struggles dismissed as character failures. The church sometimes adds another layer by attaching spiritual language to what are actually neurological experiences.

Healing from that specific kind of shame requires more than a verse about grace. It requires acknowledging that some of what you were told about yourself was simply wrong — and that recognizing that isn't bitterness. It's clarity.

You're seven years old, sitting in the principal's office again. Your teacher sent you there because you couldn't sit still during story time, you blurted out answers without raising your hand, and you got up to sharpen your pencil three times in ten minutes. The principal's voice drones on about "appropriate behavior" and "following classroom rules," but all you hear is the underlying message: you're different, you're disruptive, you're a problem.

By twelve, you've internalized the script. You're the kid who tries hard but can't seem to get it right. You forget your homework, lose your assignments, interrupt conversations, and say things that make other kids look at you strangely. Adults speak to you with that tone of patient exasperation reserved for children who should know better but somehow don't.

In high school, you watch your friends get into their dream colleges while you struggle to maintain a C average despite being obviously intelligent. Your SAT scores are inconsistent, your grades don't reflect your abilities, and your application essays ramble in directions that seem important to you but apparently don't impress admissions committees.

By adulthood, you've accumulated decades of evidence that you're fundamentally flawed. You've been fired from jobs, ended relationships, started projects you couldn't finish, and disappointed people who believed in you. The voice in your head has become your own, but it still carries the same message: you're not enough, you'll never be enough, and everyone can see it.

> ⚠ **Caution:** Don't use past failures as evidence that you can't succeed in similar situations. Your ADHD brain tends to overgeneralize negative experiences, but each attempt is independent and benefits from everything you've learned since the last try.

This is the brutal accumulation of shame that many ADHD Christians carry into their faith walk. Years of criticism, failure, and rejection have convinced you that there's something fundamentally wrong with you that no amount of effort can fix. When you encounter the gospel message of love and acceptance, it sounds too good to be true because it contradicts everything your experience has taught you about yourself.

ADHD symptoms read as moral failures to people who don't know what they're looking at. You can't focus: lazy. You interrupt: rude. You forget commitments: don't care. Struggle with organization: irresponsible. The judgments are wrong. But they accumulate anyway, building a false narrative that eventually sounds like your own voice.

> ★ **Pro Tip:** Practice the "so what, now what" response to failures. Acknowledge them quickly ("so what, I messed up") and focus on next steps ("now what can I learn or do differently"). Ruminating on failures serves no productive purpose for ADHD brains.

Rejection Sensitive Dysphoria amplifies every criticism and perceived slight until they feel like devastating indictments of your entire being. A casual comment from a coworker becomes evidence that you're incompetent. A friend's delayed response to a text message confirms that you're annoying. A spouse's suggestion for improvement feels like total rejection of who you are. Your brain takes neutral or even positive interactions and filters them through a lens of anticipated rejection.

The church environment can be triggering for ADHD shame because it emphasizes qualities that don't come naturally to your brain: consistency, self-control, quiet contemplation, systematic spiritual growth, and reliable service. When you struggle to maintain daily devotions, sit still during sermons, or follow through on ministry commitments, it's easy to conclude that you're a spiritual failure who can't access the resources that seem readily available to other believers.

> ★ **Pro Tip:** Create a "failure resume" listing your mistakes and what you learned from each one. This reframes failures as learning experiences and reduces the shame that keeps you stuck in repetitive patterns.

Shame tells a different story than guilt. Guilt says, "I did something bad." Shame says, "I am something bad." Guilt can motivate positive change because it focuses on behaviors that can be modified. Shame paralyzes because it attacks your fundamental identity and worth. For ADHD Christians, the accumulated years of shame can make it almost impossible to believe that God truly accepts and loves you as you are.

The gospel directly contradicts the shame narrative. Romans 8:1 declares that there is no condemnation for those who are in Christ Jesus. This isn't conditional love based on your performance. It's not temporary acceptance that can be withdrawn when you fail. It's permanent, unshakeable identity as God's beloved child that doesn't fluctuate based on your ADHD symptoms or their consequences.

Knowing this intellectually and believing it emotionally are two different things. Your brain has spent years collecting evidence for your fundamental unworthiness. Shame has become so familiar that it feels like truth instead of a distorted interpretation of your experiences. Challenging these deep-seated beliefs requires more than positive thinking or spiritual willpower.

> ★ Pro Tip: Develop "shame interrupts" — quick phrases that stop shame spirals before they gain momentum. "That's my ADHD brain, not my character," or "This feeling will pass," or "God's love doesn't depend on my performance."

The process of healing from shame begins with recognizing it for what it is: a lie that contradicts God's truth about your identity and worth. This recognition often comes slowly, through repeated exposure to grace and acceptance that gradually overrides the internal voice of criticism and rejection. It requires surrounding yourself with people who see your worth even when you can't see it yourself.

Failure hits ADHD brains differently than neurotypical ones because your executive function challenges make failure more frequent and your emotional intensity makes it feel more devastating. You might start projects with great enthusiasm only to lose interest when the initial excitement wears off. You might make commitments with sincere intentions but struggle to follow through when competing demands overwhelm your capacity. You might have brilliant ideas but lack the sustained focus necessary to implement them successfully.

Each failure reinforces the narrative that you can't be trusted, that you're unreliable, that you'll always let people down. This becomes a self-fulfilling prophecy as the fear of failure makes you either avoid challenges entirely or approach them with such anxiety that you sabotage your own efforts. The shame of past failures makes future success feel impossible because you've lost confidence in your own capabilities.

Learning to reframe failure is essential for ADHD emotional health. Failure isn't evidence of your fundamental inadequacy. It's information about which approaches don't work for your brain and which environments don't support your success. When you fail at something, instead of asking "What's wrong with me?" try asking "What did I learn?" and "How can I approach this differently next time?"

The biblical perspective on failure emphasizes growth, learning, and redemption instead of condemnation. Job's declaration that he will "come forth as gold" after being tested reflects the truth that difficult experiences can refine and strengthen us instead of defining our worth. Peter's denial of Jesus didn't disqualify him from leadership; it became part of his preparation for understanding grace and forgiveness.

Perfectionism often develops as a defensive response to shame and fear of failure. If you can just do everything perfectly, maybe people won't notice your underlying flaws. Maybe you can earn the acceptance that you're not sure you deserve naturally. But perfectionism is an impossible standard that sets you up for constant failure and reinforces the shame it's meant to protect against.

ADHD brains are ill-suited for perfectionism because your neurological differences make consistent performance impossible. Some days your brain will work beautifully, and you'll accomplish more than you thought possible. Other days you'll struggle to complete basic tasks despite your best efforts. Trying to maintain perfect performance with an inconsistent brain is like trying to run a marathon with a broken leg.

"Good enough" becomes a radical act of self-compassion for perfectionist ADHD minds. This doesn't mean lowering your standards or accepting mediocrity. It means recognizing that perfect is the enemy of good, and that completing something imperfectly is better than not completing it at all because you were paralyzed by perfectionist anxiety.

The comparison trap is dangerous for ADHD Christians because you're constantly measuring your performance against neurotypical standards. You see other believers maintaining consistent spiritual disciplines, serving faithfully in long-term ministries, managing their households efficiently, and achieving steady career progression. Your scattered, inconsistent, non-linear path feels like failure in comparison.

> ⚠ **Caution:** Avoid comparing your failure rate to neurotypical people's success rate. Your brain faces different challenges and requires different strategies, so your learning curve might look different without indicating anything about your potential.

God doesn't call everyone to the same path or the same pace. David's psalms reveal a spiritual path full of ups and downs, intense emotions, and dramatic swings between faith and doubt. Paul's ministry was marked by conflict, controversy, and opposition. Neither of their stories would look like success by conventional standards, yet both were used powerfully by God for His purposes.

Your ADHD experience isn't a deviation from God's plan for your life. It is God's plan for your life. The struggles, the failures, the rejections, and the shame are all part of the raw material He's using to shape you into the person He created you to be. This doesn't mean He causes your pain, but it does mean He can redeem it and use it for purposes you might not yet understand.

Healing from rejection requires learning to separate your worth from others' opinions. This is challenging for ADHD brains because your emotional intensity makes rejection feel life-threatening and your history of criticism makes you expect disapproval. But the truth is that other people's opinions about you, while they might affect your circumstances, don't determine your value or identity.

Some people will never understand or appreciate your ADHD traits. They'll see your distractibility as rudeness, your emotional intensity as drama, your creative thinking as impracticality. Their rejection hurts, but it doesn't mean they're right about you. It means they're not your people. Finding communities that appreciate neurodiversity and value your unique contributions becomes essential for emotional health.

The practice of self-compassion involves treating yourself with the same kindness and understanding you would offer a good friend facing similar struggles. When you make a mistake, instead of launching into self-attack mode, try responding with curiosity and care. What were the circumstances that contributed to this outcome? What support or resources might have helped? How can you approach similar situations differently in the future?

This self-compassion isn't self-indulgence or making excuses. It's creating the emotional safety necessary for honest self-reflection and genuine growth. Shame-based motivation might drive short-term behavior change, but it doesn't lead to lasting transformation because it attacks the person instead of addressing the behavior.

A theology of imperfection becomes crucial for ADHD Christians. The gospel isn't about becoming perfect before God will love you. It's about God loving you while you're still imperfect and working gradually to transform you into the person He created you to be. This transformation happens throughout a lifetime, not overnight, and it includes your ADHD traits instead of eliminating them.

The Japanese concept of kintsugi, the art of repairing broken pottery with gold, provides a beautiful metaphor for how God works with our brokenness. Instead of hiding the cracks or pretending they don't exist, kintsugi highlights them with precious metal, making the repaired object more beautiful than it was originally. Your struggles with ADHD, the failures and rejections you've experienced, can become the very places where God's grace shines most brightly.

Resilience against shame and rejection requires intentional practices that reinforce truth about your identity and worth. Regular reminders of God's love, affirmations of your unique gifts and contributions, celebration of small victories, and connection with supportive communities all help counteract the negative messages your brain has learned to believe about itself.

The goal isn't to eliminate all negative emotions or to become immune to criticism and failure. The goal is to develop the emotional stability and spiritual grounding necessary to experience difficult emotions without being destroyed by them. You can feel disappointed without believing you're a disappointment. You can experience rejection without concluding you're rejectable. You can fail at something without deciding you're a failure.

Your ADHD brain's history of shame, rejection, and failure doesn't have to define your future. These experiences have shaped you, but they don't limit what God can do in and through your life. The same sensitivity that makes criticism feel devastating also enables deep empathy with others who are struggling. The same intensity that makes failure feel catastrophic also fuels passionate engagement with causes you care about.

✗ Danger Zone: Avoid people who use your failures as ammunition against your character or worth. Healthy relationships see failures as learning opportunities, not identity statements, and support growth instead of highlighting shortcomings.

God specializes in using broken things for beautiful purposes. Your cracks, your struggles, your imperfections aren't obstacles to His love or barriers to His purposes. They're the very places where His grace can shine most clearly, not just in your own life but in the lives of others who need to see that it's possible to be both imperfect and deeply loved.

The path from shame to freedom is gradual and requires patience with yourself. There will be setbacks and moments when the old voices of criticism and rejection feel louder than God's voice of love and acceptance. But each time you choose truth over lies, grace over condemnation, and love over fear, you're rewiring neural pathways that have been strengthened by years of negative reinforcement.

You are not your ADHD symptoms. You are not your failures. You are not the sum of all the criticism and rejection you've experienced. You are a beloved child of God, created with intention and purpose, deserving of love and respect regardless of how well you conform to neurotypical expectations. This is not just a nice sentiment. This is the foundational truth upon which your entire identity can rest.

Part V: Thriving, Not Just Surviving

Celebrating Your ADHD Strengths

"Each of you should use whatever gift you have to serve others, as faithful stewards of God's grace in its various forms." (1 Peter 4:10, NIV)

"There are different kinds of gifts, but the same Spirit distributes them. There are different kinds of service, but the same Lord. There are different kinds of working, but in all of them and in everyone it is the same God at work." (1 Corinthians 12:4-6, NIV)

You've spent most of this book reading about the challenges, struggles, and difficulties that come with having an ADHD brain. You've probably recognized yourself in the stories of scattered attention, emotional dysregulation, rejection sensitivity, and social exhaustion. By now, you might be wondering if there's anything good about having ADHD at all, or if it's just a collection of problems to be managed and deficits to be overcome.

I didn't overcome my ADHD. I weaponized it.

The hypervigilance that years of navigating an unpredictable environment builds in ADHD brains became my edge in reading complex systems and the people inside them. The systematic thinking I developed to find patterns and impose order on chaos became the ability to design solutions that actually worked. The emotional intensity that made relationships complicated made me impossible to ignore when I had something worth saying.

What looked like damage was raw material.

This reframe isn't toxic positivity. It's not "everything happens for a reason" dressed up in different language. It's something more specific: the recognition that the coping mechanisms you built, the skills you developed to survive an environment that wasn't designed for your brain — those things are real. They transferred. They have value in contexts that have nothing to do with where they came from.

The ADHD traits that got you in trouble in school — the intensity, the pattern-recognition, the inability to pretend something boring is interesting, the need to find the real reason behind the official reason — those same traits make you valuable in a crisis, in a creative project, in a conversation with someone who needs to be told the truth. God doesn't waste the hard stuff. He has a frustrating habit of using exactly the thing that cost you the most.

Here's what nobody told you when you were sitting in that principal's office, struggling through school, or getting fired from another job: your ADHD brain is not broken. It's not a lesser version of a "normal" brain. It's not a collection of deficits wrapped in a disorder. Your ADHD brain is a different type of processor that comes equipped with some of the most powerful cognitive tools available to humanity.

✗ Danger Zone: Don't let others diminish your ADHD gifts by calling them "normal" traits everyone has. Your brain's wiring creates unique combinations and intensities of abilities that deserve recognition and appreciation.

The same neural differences that make traditional environments challenging also create extraordinary capabilities that neurotypical brains struggle to access. Your scattered attention isn't just a problem with focus—it's also the ability to notice patterns and connections that others miss. Your emotional intensity isn't just poor regulation—it's also the capacity for deep empathy and passionate engagement. Your impulsivity isn't just lack of self-control—it's also the courage to take risks and make split-second decisions that can save the day.

For decades, the entire medical and educational conversation about ADHD has been about what ADHD brains can't do. The focus never moved to what they can do extraordinarily well. That wasn't accidental — institutions measure what they can standardize, and your brain resists standardization. The result is generations of people who got very good at believing they were fundamentally broken.

★ **Pro Tip:** Ask trusted friends to help you identify your ADHD strengths. You might be blind to your own gifts because they feel natural to you, while others can see clearly how your brain's unique wiring benefits them and situations you're both in.

God doesn't make mistakes. When He created your brain with its unique wiring, He wasn't accidentally including bugs in the software. He was intentionally designing features that serve certain purposes in His kingdom. Your ADHD traits aren't obstacles to overcome—they're tools to develop and deploy for His glory and others' benefit.

I spent a long time cataloguing my deficits before I started cataloguing my assets. The deficits were easier to count — there were so many of them, and everyone around me was keeping score. The assets were harder to see because they felt like just the way I was, not like anything special. The pattern recognition I used to survive a chaotic childhood turned out to be the same skill that made me good at understanding complex systems. The emotional intensity I was told to manage turned out to be the reason people trusted me with hard conversations. None of it was designed by me. All of it turned out to be useful.

And it's worth saying the other thing too, the thing this book sometimes undersells: some ADHD Christians don't just survive church. They find a home there in ways that surprise them.

Worship is one of the places where hyperfocus becomes an asset rather than a liability. When the music connects and the message lands and the room is charged with something real, ADHD brains can go all the way in. Not performing engagement — actually present, actually moved, actually there in a way that's rare in daily life. The same intensity that makes a boring meeting feel like slow suffocation makes a meaningful worship experience feel like oxygen.

Service is another. The right ministry role — not the committee, not the weekly obligation, but the thing that actually matches how your brain fires — can be the environment where ADHD traits stop being liabilities and start being exactly what's needed. Crisis response, creative problem-solving, the ability to read a room and respond to what's actually happening rather than what was planned. Churches need those things. ADHD brains carry them.

If you haven't found that yet, it doesn't mean it isn't there. It may mean the roles you've tried haven't matched your wiring, or the church hasn't been the right fit, or the timing was wrong. The version of church that works for your brain exists. Some of you are already in it and haven't fully let yourself believe it's allowed to feel this good.

> ★ **Pro Tip:** Use your hyperfocus strategically for ministry projects. When you feel that familiar tunnel vision coming on, redirect it toward kingdom work that energizes you instead of fighting it or feeling guilty about it.

Your creative thinking abilities are another hidden superpower. While neurotypical brains tend toward linear, logical problem-solving, your brain makes unexpected connections between seemingly unrelated concepts. You see solutions that others miss because you approach problems from angles they never considered. Your mind naturally thinks in metaphors, analogies, and creative associations that can lead to innovative breakthroughs.

This creative thinking shows up everywhere once you stop apologizing for it. You explain biblical truths through contemporary analogies that actually land. You design systems nobody else thought to build. You might design systems and processes that improve efficiency by thinking outside conventional frameworks. You might see opportunities and possibilities that more linear thinkers overlook entirely.

Your ability to see the big picture while simultaneously noticing small details gives you a unique perspective on problems and situations. While others might get lost in either broad concepts or detailed minutiae, your brain can hold both simultaneously. This makes you valuable as a strategist who can envision long-term goals while also identifying the steps needed to achieve them.

Crisis management is where many ADHD brains truly shine. When emergencies arise, when plans fall apart, when unexpected challenges demand immediate response, your brain kicks into high gear in ways that can save the day. Your ability to think quickly, adapt rapidly, and make decisions under pressure becomes invaluable in situations where careful planning and systematic approaches would be too slow.

Emergency responders, crisis counselors, and disaster relief workers often display ADHD traits because these roles require exactly the kind of quick thinking and adaptability that your brain provides naturally. When others are paralyzed by unexpected circumstances, you're energized by the challenge and able to respond effectively.

Your emotional intelligence and empathy are often overlooked strengths in discussions of ADHD. The same sensitivity that makes rejection feel devastating also makes you acutely aware of others' emotional states. You can sense when someone is struggling even when they're trying to hide it. You feel others' pain deeply and respond with genuine compassion. This makes you naturally gifted at pastoral care, counseling, and any role that requires understanding and connecting with people.

Your emotional intensity, when channeled positively, becomes passionate engagement that can inspire and motivate others. When you care about something, you care completely. This depth of feeling can drive extraordinary commitment to causes, relationships, and goals that matter to you. Your enthusiasm can be contagious, helping others connect with ideas and purposes they might otherwise overlook.

★ Pro Tip: Create a "strength story" collection — examples of times your ADHD traits led to positive outcomes. Write them down with details about what happened and how your neurological differences contributed to success.

The ability to run multiple projects simultaneously is another ADHD strength that looks like a liability from the outside. You can often manage several engaging projects more effectively than a neurotypical person handles one — because variety is the stimulation, not the distraction. Your brain's restlessness drives innovation and prevents stagnation. You get bored before things calcify into mediocrity, which makes you useful in organizations that need someone to ask why before everyone else has stopped asking.

The ADHD tendency to question authority and challenge conventional wisdom can be a tremendous asset when systems need reform or traditions need updating. You might not accept "that's how we've always done it" as a sufficient reason to continue ineffective practices. Your willingness to challenge the status quo can drive positive change in organizations, communities, and ministries.

Your ability to see through facades and pretense gives you a kind of social X-ray vision that can be invaluable in leadership and counseling roles. While others might be fooled by appearances or smooth talk, your brain often picks up on inconsistencies and authenticity issues that reveal character and motivation. This discernment can protect you and others from deception and manipulation.

The ADHD brain's pattern recognition abilities are often extraordinary. You can spot trends, connections, and recurring themes that others miss because your attention naturally scans for interesting patterns instead of focusing on single points of data. This makes you valuable in research, analysis, and any field that benefits from seeing underlying structures and relationships.

The resilience you've built from years of failing, adapting, and trying again is not a soft skill. It's hard-won and specific. You know how to bounce back because you've had to. You know how to find creative solutions because the conventional ones kept not working for you. That combination — resilience plus unconventional problem-solving — is what a lot of people are looking for and can't find.

Three hours of hyperfocused work will often outperform eight hours of steady grinding. This isn't a rationalization — it's just how your brain runs. The goal isn't to force yourself into someone else's productivity schedule. It's to protect the conditions where your brain actually fires, and stop apologizing for the conditions where it doesn't.

The ADHD brain's comfort with chaos and uncertainty makes you valuable in rapidly changing environments where others might feel overwhelmed or paralyzed. You can function effectively in situations where traditional planning and systematic approaches are impossible. This adaptability is increasingly valuable in our fast-paced, constantly changing world.

Your natural inclination toward authenticity and emotional honesty can be refreshing in environments where political correctness and social performance often mask real thoughts and feelings. People often feel comfortable being genuine around you because you model vulnerability and authenticity in your own communication style.

The intense curiosity that drives ADHD brains can lead to broad knowledge bases and unexpected expertise in diverse areas. While others might specialize deeply in narrow fields, you might develop interesting competencies across multiple domains. This intellectual diversity can lead to innovative cross-pollination of ideas and approaches.

★ **Pro Tip:** Practice "strength spotting" in other ADHD people. Notice and affirm the gifts you see in fellow neurodivergent Christians. This trains your brain to recognize similar patterns in yourself and builds community connections.

Your ability to see potential in people and situations that others might write off as hopeless comes from your brain's natural optimism and pattern recognition abilities. You can envision how struggling people might succeed with the right support, how failing projects might be salvaged with creative adjustments, or how challenging circumstances might be transformed into opportunities.

The shift from deficit thinking to strength thinking isn't denial. It's accuracy. You're not pretending the hard parts don't exist. You're insisting on counting the full balance sheet instead of just the losses. Your ADHD traits are real capabilities. They were expensive to develop. They're yours.

⚠ **Caution:** Avoid using strength-focused thinking to minimize real challenges that need attention. Celebrating your creativity doesn't eliminate the need for organizational systems, and acknowledging your empathy doesn't excuse emotional dysregulation.

Paul's reminder that "we are God's handiwork, created in Christ Jesus to do good works, which God prepared in advance for us to do" applies directly to your ADHD brain. The same God who prepared good works for you to do also designed your brain with the capabilities needed to accomplish those works. Your ADHD traits aren't obstacles to your calling—they're tools designed for your purpose.

The goal isn't to become well-rounded or to excel at everything. The goal is to identify your unique combination of strengths and find ways to use them in service of God's kingdom and others' benefit. When you operate from your strengths instead of constantly trying to shore up your weaknesses, you become more effective, more fulfilled, and more aligned with how God designed you to function.

> ⚠ **Caution:** Don't swing from self-hatred to uncritical self-celebration. Balanced self-awareness acknowledges both gifts and challenges honestly, using strengths strategically while managing weaknesses responsibly.

Your ADHD brain brings gifts to the world that desperately needs them: creativity in the face of stagnation, innovation in response to outdated systems, empathy for those who are struggling, courage to take necessary risks, and the ability to see possibilities that others miss. These aren't side effects of your neurological differences—they're the main features.

Learning to celebrate your strengths doesn't mean ignoring your challenges or pretending that ADHD doesn't create real difficulties. It means developing a balanced perspective that acknowledges both the gifts and the struggles while building your identity around what you can do instead of what you can't do.

When you fully embrace and develop your ADHD strengths, you become a force for positive change in whatever environments you enter. Your different way of thinking, feeling, and engaging with the world becomes a gift to communities that might otherwise remain stuck in conventional patterns. Your ADHD brain isn't something to be ashamed of or to overcome—it's something to be celebrated, developed, and offered as your unique contribution to God's work in the world.

"Two are better than one, because they have a good return for their labor: If either of them falls down, one can help the other up. But pity anyone who falls and has no one to help them up." (Ecclesiastes 4:9-10, NIV)

"Carry each other's burdens, and in this way you will fulfill the law of Christ." (Galatians 6:2, NIV)

"As iron sharpens iron, so one person sharpens another." (Proverbs 27:17, NIV)

You're sitting in your car after another failed attempt at functioning like a normal adult. You forgot about the parent-teacher conference until you got the reminder email fifteen minutes before it started. You rushed to the school, arrived ten minutes late with mismatched shoes and coffee-stained clothes, only to discover that the meeting was scheduled for next week. The secretary's polite smile couldn't hide her judgment as you apologized for the third time this semester.

As you drive home, the familiar voice in your head starts its well-rehearsed monologue: "You can't keep it together. You're a mess. How are you supposed to parent when you can't even manage a simple calendar? Other parents don't have these problems. Maybe your kid would be better off if someone more competent was handling their education."

This is the moment when having a support system makes the difference between shame spiraling for hours and recovering with perspective intact. Instead of marinating in self-criticism, you text your ADHD mom friend: "Just showed up to a parent conference that's next week. Currently questioning my fitness for human society." Within minutes, she responds: "Last month

I went to the wrong school for my kid's play. You're not alone in this chaos."

That simple exchange does what hours of positive self-talk couldn't accomplish. It reminds you that you're not uniquely incompetent, that other people struggle with similar challenges, and that mistakes don't define your worth or capability. This is the power of intentional support systems for ADHD brains.

★ Pro Tip: Diversify your support network so no single person carries the burden of all your needs. Different people can provide different types of support more sustainably — one for practical help, another for emotional encouragement, another for spiritual guidance.

Most advice about building support networks assumes you have consistent social energy and reliable follow-through. You don't. Neither does anyone else with ADHD. Your social needs are intense but intermittent. Your capacity for emotional support varies wildly based on stress levels and life circumstances. Your executive function challenges make traditional relationship maintenance difficult.

You need people who understand why you disappear for weeks when overwhelmed. Who don't take your scattered communication personally. Who will text back "same" when you tell them you showed up to the wrong school.

ADHD-friendly support systems require three types of connections: professional support for the technical aspects of managing your brain, peer support from others who share your neurological experience, and personal support from family and friends who understand and accept your ADHD traits.

Professional support includes healthcare providers who understand ADHD beyond childhood hyperactivity stereotypes. You need doctors who recognize that ADHD affects adults differently than children and that symptoms change throughout your lifetime. You need therapists who understand the intersection of ADHD and mental health, who can help you develop coping strategies that work with your brain instead of against it.

Finding ADHD-competent professionals requires more research than it should. Many healthcare providers received minimal training on adult ADHD, especially how it presents in women and minorities. Don't settle for dismissive attitudes or outdated information. A provider who still thinks ADHD is a childhood condition you outgrow is not the provider you need.

Peer support from other ADHD adults provides something non-ADHD people can't give you, no matter how much they love you. Other ADHD adults don't need the explanation. They already know what it costs to lose two hours to a Wikipedia spiral, to start ten projects and finish none, to feel like everyone else was handed a manual for basic adulting that somehow got lost in the mail before yours arrived.

Local ADHD support groups offer face-to-face connection and community resources. Many areas have groups for adults, parents of ADHD children, or women with ADHD. These groups can provide practical tips, emotional support, and advocacy opportunities.

Be cautious about support groups that focus primarily on complaints and problems without offering solutions or hope. While venting can be therapeutic, groups that reinforce victim mentality or learned helplessness can be counterproductive. Look for communities that balance acknowledgment of challenges with celebration of strengths and practical problem-solving.

Personal support from family and friends requires education and communication about what ADHD is and how it affects your daily life. Many people still think ADHD is just childhood hyperactivity that you should have outgrown. They might not understand why you can't just try harder, pay attention, or remember important things.

> ★ **Pro Tip:** Be clear about support needs when asking for help. Instead of "I'm struggling," try "I need someone to help me organize my paperwork for an hour" or "I need to talk through this decision with someone who won't judge my scattered thinking."

Sharing accurate information about ADHD can help loved ones understand that your challenges are neurological, not character-based. Books, articles, and videos about ADHD can provide context that helps family members respond with compassion instead of frustration when you struggle with executive function tasks.

Setting realistic expectations becomes crucial for maintaining supportive relationships. Help people understand what you can and can't reliably do, what accommodations help you function better, and how they can support you without enabling dependency. This might mean asking for help with organization while maintaining responsibility for decision-making or requesting deadline reminders while still owning the consequences of missed deadlines.

Your support team starts with identifying the types of help you need and matching them with appropriate people. You might need someone who can provide accountability for important tasks, someone who offers emotional support during difficult times, someone who helps with practical problem-solving, and someone who can provide perspective when your thinking gets distorted.

> ★ **Pro Tip:** Build reciprocal relationships by offering your ADHD strengths to others. Your crisis management skills, creative problem-solving, or emotional intuition might be exactly what someone else needs, even when your organization skills aren't helpful.

Don't expect any single person to meet all your support needs. That's unfair to them and unrealistic for you. Diversify your support network so that different people provide different types of assistance. This prevents burnout in your supporters and ensures that help is available even when some team members are unavailable.

Reciprocal support strengthens relationships and prevents you from feeling like a burden. Your ADHD brain brings unique gifts to friendships: creativity, empathy, crisis management skills, and passionate engagement. Look for ways to contribute to others' lives that use your strengths instead of requiring your areas of weakness.

You might not be reliable for regular check-ins or organized support, but you might be excellent at providing encouragement during crises, creative problem-solving, or helping people see possibilities they missed. Recognize and offer your unique contributions to balance the support you receive.

Communication about your needs requires ongoing conversation instead of one-time explanations. Your ADHD symptoms and support needs might change based on stress levels, life circumstances, medication adjustments, or new insights about your brain. Keep supporters updated about what's working and what isn't so they can adjust their approach accordingly.

Boundary setting protects both you and your supporters from burnout and resentment. Be clear about what you can offer in terms of emotional availability, time commitments, and reciprocal support. Don't overpromise in moments of gratitude or guilt, and don't feel obligated to accept help that comes with conditions you can't meet.

Some people won't be able to provide the support you need, and that's okay. Not everyone has the capacity, understanding, or willingness to accommodate ADHD-related challenges. It's not your job to educate everyone or to maintain relationships with people who consistently respond to your struggles with criticism or dismissal.

⚠ **Caution:** Don't expect neurotypical friends to intuitively understand ADHD needs without clear communication. Good intentions don't automatically translate to effective support, and education prevents frustration on both sides.

Crisis support planning helps ensure that assistance is available during your most vulnerable moments. Identify who you can call when you're overwhelmed, struggling with mental health symptoms, or facing urgent practical problems. Have backup options in case your primary supports aren't available.

Develop safety plans for managing suicidal thoughts, severe depression, or other mental health crises that might accompany ADHD struggles. Know the warning signs that indicate you need professional intervention and have contact information readily available for crisis hotlines, emergency services, or mental health professionals.

⚠ **Caution:** Avoid becoming dependent on others for basic functioning without working toward sustainable independence. Support should enhance your capabilities, not replace your agency and responsibility for your own life.

Support systems are an ongoing process instead of a one-time task. Your needs will change as you grow, as circumstances shift, and as you develop new coping skills. Stay open to new connections while maintaining the relationships that have proven valuable.

Solomon's wisdom in Ecclesiastes reminds us that "two are better than one" and that we need others to help us up when we fall. This isn't just nice sentiment—it's practical reality for ADHD brains that face unique challenges and need understanding support to thrive.

Your ADHD brain wasn't designed to function in isolation. The same traits that create challenges also create opportunities for deep connection with others who understand your experience. Building intentional support systems isn't admitting weakness—it's acknowledging the reality that we all need community to become the people God created us to be.

> **✗ Danger Zone:** Avoid making your ADHD everyone else's responsibility to manage. Support means help, not rescue, and healthy relationships maintain appropriate boundaries around who owns which problems and solutions.

The right support system doesn't fix your ADHD. It changes what your ADHD costs you. That's the difference between managing alone — which is exhausting and mostly unsuccessful — and managing with people who know what they're dealing with and have agreed to help anyway. Solomon was right. Two are better than one. For ADHD brains especially, that's not sentiment. It's strategy.

Parenting and Legacy

It's 7:23 AM on a Tuesday, and you're standing in the kitchen wearing yesterday's shirt because you forgot to do laundry again. Your eight-year-old is having a meltdown because the cereal box is the wrong color (you accidentally bought the store brand), your five-year-old can't find matching socks, and you just realized that today is picture day at school. The permission slip for the field trip that was due yesterday is still buried somewhere in the disaster zone you call a dining room table.

Your spouse left early for work, and you're facing another morning of solo parenting while your brain feels like it's wrapped in cotton. You know you should have prepared everything the night before, but last night you hyperfocused on organizing the junk drawer until midnight instead of packing lunches or laying out clothes. Now everyone is going to be late, stressed, and probably wearing mismatched outfits in their school pictures.

As you frantically search for clean socks while simultaneously trying to calm a crying child and remember whether you signed the reading log, that familiar voice starts its commentary: "Real parents have their act together. Other families don't live in constant chaos. Your kids deserve better than this disorganized mess you call parenting."

Parenting with ADHD means your best intentions collide daily with your executive function. You'll create magical moments and complete disasters, sometimes in the same afternoon. The question you'll ask yourself most often: are you screwing up your kids, or giving them something a neurotypical parent couldn't?

ADHD parenting is a study in contradictions. You can spend three hours building an elaborate fort with your children, completely absorbed in their imaginative play, then forget to give them lunch until 3 PM. You can provide profound emotional support during their crises while struggling to maintain basic household routines. You can be the parent who notices when they're struggling emotionally while missing obvious signs that they need new shoes.

Traditional parenting books were not written for you. They assume consistent executive function, predictable energy, and routines that hold under pressure. None of them account for brains that forget important events, get overwhelmed by sensory chaos, or need recovery time after three hours with small humans who have no volume control whatsoever.

★ **Pro Tip:** Model self-compassion about your ADHD struggles so your children learn to treat their own differences with kindness. Your children watch how you handle your imperfections more closely than your successes, and they'll internalize your self-talk patterns.

ADHD parenting has a flip side. Your neurological differences create real strengths for your children — things conventional parenting doesn't provide. Your emotional intensity enables deep empathy with your children's struggles. Your creativity brings magic to ordinary moments. Your ability to hyperfocus can create extraordinary experiences when something captures your interest. Your willingness to challenge conventional wisdom can help you advocate for your children when systems don't serve them well.

Parent from your strengths. Build systems for the rest. And drop the perfectionist parenting ideal entirely — it was never designed for your brain.

One of the real gifts of ADHD parenting is what you model. Whether your children are neurodivergent or not, they grow up watching a parent who demonstrates that different brains work differently and that neurological diversity is normal instead of problematic.

If your children have inherited ADHD traits, you can provide understanding and advocacy that neurotypical parents might struggle to offer. You know what it feels like to be constantly corrected for behaviors you can't easily control. You understand the shame of forgetting important things despite caring deeply. You recognize the exhaustion that comes from trying to fit into systems designed for different brains.

> ⚠ **Caution:** Don't assume your children have ADHD just because you do, but don't dismiss signs that suggest evaluation. ADHD has genetic components but isn't automatically inherited, and each child deserves assessment based on their individual presentation.

This experiential knowledge can help you respond to your children's ADHD symptoms with compassion instead of frustration. Instead of seeing their scattered attention as defiance, you can recognize it as a neurological difference that needs accommodation. Instead of interpreting their emotional intensity as manipulation, you can validate their feelings while teaching regulation skills.

Even neurotypical kids benefit from growing up with a neurodivergent parent. They learn early that brains work differently and that different isn't a ranking. They develop flexibility from living in a house that doesn't run on conventional rhythms. They get a parent who takes their interior life seriously because you know what it's like to have your interior life dismissed.

Your emotional intensity creates real connection with your kids when it's channeled right. When you're fully present and engaged, you can provide the kind of attention and enthusiasm that makes childhood memories. You get excited about the things they're excited about. You see wonder in small things because you still have access to that frequency. That's not nothing. That's actually rare.

This same emotional intensity can also be overwhelming for children, especially during your dysregulated moments. Learning to recognize when your emotions are too big for the situation and developing strategies for regulation becomes crucial for healthy parenting. Your children need to see that adults can have big feelings without being controlled by them.

The ADHD tendency to hyperfocus can create incredible parenting moments when directed toward your children. You might spend hours building elaborate Lego creations, reading entire book series together, or exploring nature in exhaustive detail. These experiences of having a parent's complete, undivided attention can be powerful gifts.

Hyperfocus cuts both ways as a parent. When it's pointed at your kids it creates extraordinary moments. When it pulls you into a project at midnight while lunches aren't packed and permission slips aren't signed, it's the thing everyone in the house pays for the next morning. External accountability systems aren't optional — they're how you protect your family from the cost of your own absorption.

Being aware of your hyperfocus patterns and creating external accountability systems can help you channel this trait beneficially while preventing it from interfering with essential parenting functions.

Executive function challenges create some of the most visible struggles in ADHD parenting. You might consistently forget permission slips, school events, and appointment times. You might struggle to maintain household routines, meal planning, and organizational systems. You might find it difficult to follow through consistently on discipline or to maintain the structure that children need.

These challenges don't make you a bad parent, but they do require creative solutions. Building external systems that compensate for internal executive function struggles becomes essential. This might mean using multiple calendars, setting up automatic reminders, creating visual schedules for the family, or asking for help with tasks that consistently overwhelm you.

Perfectionist guilt can be brutal for ADHD parents because the gap between your intentions and your execution is often visible and frustrating. You know what good parenting looks like, you want to provide it for your children, but your brain doesn't always cooperate with your best intentions.

> ★ **Pro Tip:** Create family systems that work for ADHD brains instead of fighting your neurology daily. Use visual schedules, establish routines that don't require perfect executive function, and build flexibility into expectations so the whole family can thrive.

Learning to separate good-enough parenting from perfect parenting becomes crucial for your mental health and your family's wellbeing. Your children don't need perfect parents. They need parents who love them, who are working to grow and improve, and who can model how to handle mistakes with grace and learning.

The chaos that often characterizes ADHD households isn't necessarily harmful to children if it's balanced with love, safety, and emotional security. Some of the most creative, adaptable, resilient children come from families that operate outside conventional organizational patterns.

Time management challenges affect ADHD parenting in predictable ways. You might consistently run late for school pickup, forget about scheduled activities, or struggle to balance work demands with family time. These issues can create stress for your children and guilt for you.

Adding buffer time to your schedule, using multiple reminder systems, and communicating honestly with your children about time challenges can help minimize the impact of these struggles. Teaching your children to be flexible and to help with time management can also turn your challenges into opportunities for them to develop responsibility and problem-solving skills.

Sensory overwhelm is a common experience for ADHD parents, especially those with young children. The constant noise, mess, and physical demands of parenting can push your nervous system past its capacity for regulation. When you're overstimulated, you're more likely to react poorly to normal childhood behaviors.

Knowing your sensory limits and building in recovery time becomes essential for sustainable parenting. This might mean taking breaks when possible, creating quiet spaces in your home, using noise-canceling headphones during chaotic times, or asking for help when you're approaching overload.

The unpredictability of ADHD symptoms can make consistent parenting challenging. You might be patient and creative one day, then irritable and scattered the next. Your children might not understand why mom or dad seems different from day to day, which can create anxiety or confusion.

Age-appropriate communication about your ADHD can help children understand that your variable moods and energy levels aren't their fault. You can explain that sometimes your brain works differently and that you're working to manage these differences while still being a good parent.

⚠ **Caution:** Avoid projecting your ADHD shame onto your children's struggles. Their challenges might be similar to yours, but they're living in a different generation with different awareness and resources. Don't let your baggage become their burden.

Your children's executive function skills require intentional effort, especially if you struggle with these areas yourself. This might mean creating visual schedules, teaching organizational systems, practicing problem-solving skills, or explicitly discussing strategies for managing time and responsibilities.

Family systems that work for your ADHD brain benefit everyone in the household. This might mean having designated places for important items, establishing simple routines that don't require complex decision-making, or building flexibility into your schedule to accommodate the unexpected.

★ **Pro Tip:** Celebrate neurodivergent wins in your family. Notice when someone's ADHD traits contribute positively to family life and name it: "Your ability to notice details helped us find the lost keys" or "Your creativity made that project so much more fun."

Legacy building for ADHD parents extends beyond traditional measures of success. Your legacy might not be perfectly organized photo albums or pristine baby books. It might be children who are comfortable with neurodiversity, who know how to adapt when plans change, who understand that love isn't dependent on performance, and who have experienced the magic that comes from living with a parent whose brain works differently.

The biblical instruction to "train children in the way they should go" takes on special meaning for ADHD parents. This doesn't mean forcing your children into neurotypical molds or trying to parent according to standards that don't fit your family. It means understanding how each child is uniquely designed and providing guidance that honors their individual gifts and challenges.

Your ADHD traits, when channeled positively, can create a family culture that values creativity, authenticity, empathy, and resilience. Your children can learn that it's okay to be different, that challenges can be overcome with support and strategies, and that love is unconditional even when behavior needs correction.

The legacy you're building isn't about perfect parenting—it's about authentic relationship. Your children will remember the times you got down on the floor and played with them for hours, the creative solutions you found to problems, the way you understood their struggles, and the unconditional love you provided even when everything else felt chaotic.

Parenting with ADHD requires courage, creativity, and compassion for yourself and your children. It means abandoning perfectionist ideals in favor of authentic connection. It means building systems that work for your brain while teaching your children to navigate a world that often rewards neurotypical patterns.

Your ADHD brain wasn't a mistake in God's plan for your family. It's a unique design that brings certain gifts to your parenting experience. When you learn to parent from your strengths while managing your challenges, you create a family environment where all kinds of brains can thrive and where love matters more than performance.

> ✗ **Danger Zone:** Avoid using your ADHD as an excuse for inconsistent parenting that harms your children. They need stability and predictability even when your brain craves chaos, and your challenges don't absolve you of responsibility for their wellbeing.

The legacy isn't the organized photo albums or the consistent bedtimes or the permission slips filed on time. It's the kid who grew up watching a parent take their own brain seriously, ask for help without shame, and keep showing up even when it was hard. That's the inheritance worth leaving.

Part VI: Special Considerations

When ADHD Comes with Autism (AuDHD)

"For just as each of us has one body with many members, and these members do not all have the same function, so in Christ we, though many, form one body, and each member belongs to all the others." (Romans 12:4-5, NIV)

"But God has put the body together, giving greater honor to the parts that lacked it, so that there should be no division in the body, but that its parts should have equal concern for each other." (1 Corinthians 12:24-25, NIV)

"He has made everything beautiful in its time." (Ecclesiastes 3:11, NIV)

You're at a church social event, standing near the snack table because it gives you something to do with your hands and a reason to avoid extended eye contact. The fluorescent lights are buzzing at a frequency that makes your skin crawl, someone's perfume is triggering a headache, and the overlapping conversations create a wall of noise that your brain can't filter into individual voices.

Your ADHD brain craves social connection and new experiences, but your autistic brain is overwhelmed by the sensory chaos and unpredictable social dynamics. You want to join the animated discussion about the upcoming missions trip, but you're paralyzed by uncertainty about when to speak, how loud to be, and whether your contributions will be appropriate. Your heart races with social anxiety while your mind simultaneously buzzes with excitement about the topic.

Someone approaches and asks how you're doing. Your ADHD impulsivity wants to launch into a detailed explanation of your current special interest, but your autistic masking instincts kick in and you respond with a generic "Fine, thanks" while internally screaming at the lost opportunity for genuine connection. You spend the rest of the evening replaying this interaction, analyzing what you should have said differently.

> ★ **Pro Tip:** Learn to distinguish between ADHD overwhelm and autistic overload to choose appropriate coping strategies. ADHD overwhelm might need movement and stimulation, while autistic overload might need stillness and reduced input. Different problems need different solutions.

This is life with AuDHD—the combination of ADHD and autism that creates a unique neurological profile with its own distinct challenges and gifts. You're not ADHD-plus or autism-lite. You're both, simultaneously, and the combination creates a third thing that neither diagnostic framework fully describes.

For decades, medical understanding assumed that ADHD and autism were mutually exclusive conditions. If you had one, you couldn't have the other. This meant that countless people, especially women and girls, went undiagnosed or misdiagnosed because their presentations didn't match the stereotypical profiles of either condition alone.

Now we understand that ADHD and autism frequently co-occur, creating a neurological combination that's both more complex and more common than previously recognized. Some estimates suggest that up to 50-70% of autistic people also have ADHD traits, and 20-50% of people with ADHD also have autistic characteristics.

The internal conflicts are real and exhausting. Your ADHD wants novelty; your autism wants routine. Your ADHD fires off impulsive responses; your autism needs processing time before it can respond to anything. Your ADHD feels everything loudly; your autism is trying to regulate all that noise. You're not confused or inconsistent. You're managing two neurotypes with genuinely competing needs.

These aren't contradictory disorders fighting for control of your brain. They're two aspects of the same design, creating a cognitive profile that doesn't fit neatly into either diagnostic box. Knowing how these traits interact can help you develop strategies that honor both aspects of your neurodivergence instead of forcing you to choose between them.

★ **Pro Tip:** Create "AuDHD accommodation cards" that explain your needs in different situations. "I need movement breaks but also quiet spaces" or "I love social connection but need advance notice about plans" helps others understand your seemingly contradictory requirements.

Sensory processing with AuDHD is a negotiation that never fully resolves. Your ADHD brain seeks stimulation — loud music, movement, intense input. Your autistic brain gets overwhelmed by those same things. You might love concerts and need noise-canceling headphones for them. You might crave social gatherings and require a quiet room every forty-five minutes. The needs aren't contradictory. They just belong to different parts of a brain that are both running at once.

Social life with AuDHD is where the contradictions are most visible. You want connection — genuinely, intensely. And you exhaust yourself trying to get it. Your ADHD impulsivity overrides your awareness of timing. Your autistic brain processes language literally in a world that communicates mostly in implication. You show up wanting to connect and leave wondering what just happened.

⚠ **Caution:** Avoid masking one condition to appear more like the other. Suppressing your autistic traits to seem more stereotypically ADHD (or vice versa) depletes your energy and prevents authentic self-expression.

This combination can create painful social experiences where you desperately want connection but struggle to achieve it successfully. You might interrupt conversations because your

ADHD impulsivity overrides your awareness of social timing. You might miss sarcasm or implied meanings because your autistic brain processes language literally. You might share too much personal information because your ADHD emotional intensity overwhelms your autistic understanding of social boundaries.

The masking that many autistic people use to appear neurotypical becomes even more complex when you also have ADHD traits to manage. You're not just hiding your autistic differences—you're also trying to control your ADHD behaviors while maintaining the cognitive load of social performance. This triple burden can lead to rapid burnout and emotional exhaustion.

Executive function with AuDHD involves managing both ADHD's scattered attention and autism's need for structure and routine. Your ADHD brain struggles with planning, organization, and follow-through. Your autistic brain needs predictable routines and clear structures to function well. These needs can support each other when you use autistic systematizing to create ADHD-friendly routines, or they can conflict when your ADHD impulsivity disrupts your autistic need for predictability.

> ★ Pro Tip: Build your identity around being AuDHD instead of trying to fit into either autism or ADHD communities exclusively. You're not "not autistic enough" or "not ADHD enough" - you're uniquely both, and that combination has its own strengths and challenges.

Executive function strategies that work for both aspects of your neurodivergence requires understanding which challenges come from which source. ADHD-related executive function issues might respond to external motivation, novelty, and flexibility. Autism-related executive function challenges might respond to clear structures, predictable routines, and reduced uncertainty.

Special interests—the intense, focused passions that characterize autism—interact in complex ways with ADHD hyperfocus. When your special interest aligns with your hyperfocus, you can achieve extraordinary levels of expertise and productivity. You might spend months or years diving deep into subjects that fascinate you, developing knowledge and skills that surpass those of typical enthusiasts.

ADHD's need for novelty can also disrupt autistic special interests. You might abandon long-term interests when they stop providing sufficient stimulation, or you might struggle to maintain focus on your special interests when other activities compete for your attention. This can create guilt and confusion about whether you're "really" autistic if your interests aren't as stable as stereotypical presentations suggest.

Communication differences with AuDHD can be challenging because autism and ADHD affect language use in different ways. Your autistic brain might prefer direct, literal communication and struggle with subtext and implied meanings. Your ADHD brain might be impulsive in conversation, interrupt frequently, or go off on tangential topics that seem related to you but confusing to others.

You might be simultaneously too blunt and too scattered in your communication style. You might miss social cues while also providing too much information. You might struggle to follow conversational threads while also dominating discussions about topics that interest you.

Emotional regulation with AuDHD involves managing both ADHD's emotional intensity and autism's difficulty processing and expressing emotions. Your ADHD brain might experience emotions as overwhelming, immediate, and all-consuming. Your autistic brain might struggle to identify what emotions you're experiencing, why you're having them, or how to communicate about them effectively.

This combination can create emotional experiences that are both intense and confusing. You might have strong emotional reactions that you can't understand or explain. You might know that you're upset but be unable to identify whether you're angry, frustrated, disappointed, or overwhelmed. You might want to communicate about your emotions but lack the vocabulary or social skills to do so effectively.

> **⚠ Caution:** Don't try to manage both conditions with strategies designed for just one. You need integrated approaches that accommodate both neurotypes simultaneously, which might require creativity and professional guidance to develop.

Meltdowns and shutdowns can be more complex with AuDHD because they can be triggered by either ADHD overwhelm or autistic sensory/emotional overload. ADHD-triggered overwhelm might involve emotional dysregulation, impulsive behavior, or scattered thinking. Autism-triggered overload might involve sensory overwhelm, communication shutdown, or rigid behavior patterns.

Knowing which type of overwhelm you're experiencing can help you choose appropriate coping strategies. ADHD overwhelm might respond to movement, novelty, or emotional expression. Autistic overload might respond to reduced stimulation, predictable environments, or quiet processing time.

The church environment can be challenging for AuDHD people because it often involves the sensory, social, and cognitive demands that are most difficult for this neurological combination. Church services might include unpredictable elements, sensory overwhelm from music and crowds, social expectations for interaction, and abstract spiritual concepts that can be difficult to process literally.

Your ADHD brain might be drawn to the community aspects of church life while your autistic brain is overwhelmed by the social demands. You might be passionate about theological concepts while struggling to engage with the metaphorical language often used in sermons and worship songs. You might want to serve in ministry while being overwhelmed by the executive function demands of most volunteer roles.

Finding ways to engage with your faith community that honor both aspects of your neurodivergence becomes essential for spiritual growth and community belonging. This might mean advocating for sensory accommodations, seeking roles that match your strengths and interests, or finding quieter ways to connect with spiritual community.

Workplace challenges with AuDHD often involve managing conflicting needs around stimulation, social interaction, and structure. You might need variety and stimulation to keep your ADHD brain engaged while also needing predictability and routine to keep your autistic brain regulated. You might be naturally creative and innovative while also struggling with change and uncertainty.

Career choices become important because you need work environments that can accommodate both your need for novelty and your need for structure. This might mean finding roles that involve routine tasks with occasional variety, working in organizations that appreciate neurodivergent thinking, or creating self-employment opportunities that allow you to control your environment and schedule.

Relationships with AuDHD require partners, friends, and family members who can understand and accommodate seemingly contradictory needs. You might need both social connection and alone time, both routine and spontaneity, both emotional intimacy and space to process. These needs aren't inconsistent—they're the natural result of having a brain that operates according to two different neurological patterns.

Successful relationships require communication about your needs and the flexibility to accommodate both aspects of your neurodivergence. This might mean having regular social time balanced with predictable alone time, maintaining routines that provide stability while allowing flexibility for spontaneous activities, or developing communication styles that work for both your direct autistic preferences and your emotionally expressive ADHD traits.

> **✕ Danger Zone:** Avoid spaces that accept one part of your neurodivergence while rejecting the other. You need communities that embrace your whole neurological profile, not just the parts that are easier to understand or accommodate.

Identity formation with AuDHD can be complex because you might not fit neatly into either autistic or ADHD communities. You might feel "not autistic enough" for autism spaces because of your ADHD sociability and emotional expressiveness. You might feel "not ADHD enough" for ADHD communities because of your autistic need for routine and your processing differences.

AuDHD is a valid and distinct neurological profile can help you develop a cohesive sense of identity that honors both aspects of your neurodivergence. You don't have to choose between being autistic or having ADHD—you can be both simultaneously, with all the complexity and uniqueness that this combination brings.

Strengths of AuDHD often involve the unique combination of autistic deep thinking and ADHD creative thinking. You might be able to develop innovative solutions to complex problems by combining systematic autistic analysis with creative ADHD brainstorming. Your special interests might benefit from ADHD's ability to make unexpected connections across different domains of knowledge.

Your AuDHD brain might be gifted at seeing patterns that others miss, developing expertise in areas that fascinate you, creating systematic approaches to creative problems, or finding innovative solutions to challenges that affect neurodivergent communities.

The biblical concept of the body of Christ having many different members with different functions speaks directly to the AuDHD experience. Your neurological combination isn't a design flaw or a mistake—it's a unique configuration that serves certain purposes in God's kingdom. The traits that make you feel different or difficult in conventional settings might be exactly what's needed to address challenges that neurotypical approaches can't solve.

Paul's reminder that God gives "greater honor to the parts that lacked it" suggests that the very aspects of your neurodivergence that feel most challenging might be the ones that are most valuable to the broader community. Your AuDHD brain brings perspectives, capabilities, and insights that are essential for the health and growth of the body of Christ.

Accepting your AuDHD identity means recognizing that you don't have to choose between your autistic and ADHD traits. You can develop strategies that honor both aspects of your neurodivergence, build relationships that accommodate your complex needs, and find ways to use your unique neurological combination in service of God's kingdom and others' benefit.

Your AuDHD brain is beautifully and purposefully made, designed by a God who values diversity and uses different kinds of minds for different kinds of work. Learning to celebrate and steward this unique neurological gift is part of your calling as a beloved child of God who has been fearfully and wonderfully made.

Introversion and Overstimulation

"Be still, and know that I am God; I will be exalted among the nations, I will be exalted in the earth." (Psalm 46:10, NIV)

"But Jesus often withdrew to lonely places and prayed." (Luke 5:16, NIV)

"In repentance and rest is your salvation, in quietness and trust is your strength, but you would have none of it." (Isaiah 30:15, NIV)

It's Sunday afternoon, and you're sitting in your car in the church parking lot, unable to summon the energy to drive home. The morning service was beautiful, genuinely meaningful worship, a sermon that spoke to your heart, conversations with people you care about. But now your nervous system feels like it's been plugged into a high-voltage electrical outlet for three hours straight.

Your ADHD brain was stimulated by the music, engaged by the message, and energized by the social connections. But your introverted system is completely depleted by the same experiences that your ADHD found rewarding. The combination of sensory input, social interaction, and emotional processing has left you feeling simultaneously satisfied and utterly drained.

You know you should go to lunch with the small group like you promised, but the thought of more conversation, more decisions about what to order, more sensory input from a crowded restaurant feels impossible. You text your apologies, drive home in silence, and spend the rest of the day in your bedroom with the curtains drawn, feeling guilty about your social withdrawal but desperate for the quiet your system craves.

This is the paradox of being an introverted person with ADHD. Your brain needs stimulation to function well, but your personality needs solitude to recharge. Your ADHD symptoms might improve in stimulating environments, but your introversion requires low-stimulation recovery time. You're constantly navigating the tension between your neurological needs for engagement and your temperamental needs for quiet processing.

★ **Pro Tip:** Schedule recovery time immediately after stimulating events instead of waiting until you're depleted. Block out quiet time following church services, social gatherings, or intense work periods. Prevention is more effective than recovery for introverted ADHD brains.

Most discussions of ADHD focus on the hyperactive, extroverted presentations that are easier to spot and diagnose. The quieter, more internal experiences of introverted ADHD people often go unrecognized or misunderstood. You might be labeled as shy, antisocial, or unmotivated when you're struggling with overstimulation and introversion fatigue.

Introversion isn't about disliking people. It's about the cost of people. Introverts pay a higher stimulation price for the same social experience, and they need quiet time to pay it back down. Extroverts tend to be less sensitive to stimulation and gain energy from social interaction and external stimulation.

When you combine introversion with ADHD, you get a brain that needs stimulation to focus but becomes overwhelmed by too much stimulation. You might need background noise to concentrate but also need silence to decompress. You might crave social connection but find group interactions exhausting. You might be drawn to exciting activities but need significant recovery time afterward.

This creates a relationship with stimulation that doesn't fit the standard ADHD profile — and that gets you misread constantly. You might appear to have mild ADHD symptoms because you've learned to avoid overstimulating situations, or your symptoms might only emerge in certain contexts where your introversion allows you to access your natural ADHD energy.

Overstimulation for introverted ADHD brains can come from sources that neurotypical people or extroverted ADHD people might not even notice. Open office environments, background conversations, visual clutter, social obligations, and decision-making demands can all contribute to a sense of overwhelm that makes it difficult to function effectively.

The modern world seems designed for extroverted nervous systems, with constant connectivity, open collaboration, and high-stimulation environments. As an introverted ADHD person, you're trying to function in a world that provides both too much stimulation for your introversion and not the right kind of stimulation for your ADHD.

> ★ **Pro Tip:** Create a "social energy budget" for each week and track your expenditures like you would money. High-stimulation events cost more energy than low-key gatherings, and you can make conscious choices about how to invest your limited social resources.

Church environments can be challenging because they often involve the types of stimulation that are most difficult for introverted ADHD people: social interaction, sensory input from music and crowds, emotional processing from worship and teaching, and decision-making about participation and engagement. The very activities that are meant to be spiritually nourishing can become sources of overwhelm.

Your ADHD brain might be genuinely engaged by worship music, but your introverted system becomes overwhelmed by the volume and intensity. You might want to participate in small group discussions, but the combination of social interaction and cognitive processing exhausts your mental resources. You might appreciate fellowship opportunities but need recovery time that other church members don't seem to require.

This can create a sense of spiritual inadequacy when you can't participate in church activities with the same enthusiasm and endurance as extroverted members. You might wonder if your need for quiet reflection means you're less committed to community or if your social limitations indicate spiritual immaturity.

Jesus modeled the importance of withdrawal and solitude throughout His ministry. Luke 5:16 notes that He "often withdrew to lonely places and prayed." This wasn't escapism or antisocial behavior—it was necessary restoration that enabled sustained ministry. Even the Son of God recognized the need for quiet processing time away from the demands of crowds and disciples.

Your need for solitude and quiet isn't a spiritual weakness or a character flaw. It's a necessary part of how God designed your temperament to function. The strength that Isaiah 30:15 promises comes through "quietness and trust" isn't available to everyone in the same way, but it might be accessible to introverted temperaments.

Psalm 46:10's instruction to "be still and know that I am God" might feel more natural to your introverted system than it does to extroverted personalities. Your tendency toward internal processing and reflection can become a spiritual strength when directed toward contemplation, prayer, and meditation.

Energy management becomes crucial for introverted ADHD people because you're working with limited social and sensory resources that need careful allocation. Unlike extroverts who gain energy from social interaction, you expend energy in social situations and need to budget accordingly.

⚠ Caution: Don't use introversion as an excuse to avoid all social spiritual practices. Some connection is necessary for spiritual growth and mental health — the goal is finding sustainable ways to engage, not complete isolation.

This might mean limiting your social commitments to the ones that are most important or meaningful. It might mean building recovery time into your schedule after stimulating activities. It might mean saying no to opportunities that overwhelm your system, even when they seem beneficial or enjoyable.

Learning to recognize your early warning signs of overstimulation can help you take breaks before you become completely depleted. You might notice that you start losing your words, feeling irritable, or having difficulty making decisions when you're approaching your stimulation limits.

Social batteries are a concept that many introverts find helpful for understanding their energy limitations. Imagine that you start each day with a finite amount of social energy stored in a battery. Every social interaction, every decision you have to make, every sensory input draws power from this battery. When it's depleted, you need quiet time to recharge.

ADHD can both drain your social battery faster (because of the extra cognitive load required to manage symptoms in social situations) and make it harder to recognize when your battery is running low (because of difficulties with self-awareness and internal monitoring).

> ★ **Pro Tip:** Develop "stealth recovery" techniques for social situations when you can't leave but need to recharge. Bathroom breaks for deep breathing, stepping outside for fresh air, or finding quiet corners can provide mini-recoveries that extend your social capacity.

Being aware of your social battery level and learning to conserve energy for the interactions that matter most can help you function more sustainably in social environments. This might mean limiting small talk to save energy for meaningful conversations, or taking breaks during long social events to prevent complete depletion.

Sensory processing differences affect how quickly you become overstimulated and what types of environments feel comfortable or overwhelming. Your ADHD brain might crave certain types of sensory input while your introverted system becomes overwhelmed by others.

You might find that you can handle intense visual stimulation but are quickly overwhelmed by auditory input. You might enjoy physical movement but become exhausted by social stimulation. You might be able to focus better with background noise but need complete silence for emotional processing.

Knowing your sensory profile can help you create environments that provide the right amount and type of stimulation for both your ADHD and introversion needs. This might involve using noise-canceling headphones in busy environments, seeking out quiet spaces for work or study, or limiting your exposure to overwhelming sensory inputs.

The myth of the antisocial ADHD person often stems from misunderstanding introverted ADHD presentations. You might appear disinterested in social activities when you're managing overstimulation. You might seem unfriendly when you're conserving social energy. You might appear unmotivated when you're protecting your limited resources.

Distinguishing between social anxiety, introversion, and ADHD overwhelm can help you understand your responses to social situations more accurately. Social anxiety involves fear of social judgment or rejection. Introversion involves energy depletion from social interaction. ADHD overwhelm involves cognitive overload from managing symptoms in stimulating environments.

⚠ **Caution:** Avoid pushing through severe overstimulation without recovery because you think you "should" be able to handle more. Your limits are real and ignoring them leads to burnout that affects every area of your life.

These experiences can overlap and interact in complex ways, but understanding the different components can help you develop appropriate coping strategies. Social anxiety might respond to gradual exposure and cognitive restructuring. Introversion might be managed through energy conservation and recovery time. ADHD overwhelm might be addressed through environmental modifications and symptom management strategies.

Masking becomes exhausting for introverted ADHD people because it requires both social energy and cognitive resources to maintain. You're not just hiding your ADHD symptoms—you're also pushing your introverted system beyond its comfortable limits while maintaining a socially acceptable facade.

The combination of social performance, symptom management, and overstimulation can lead to rapid burnout and emotional exhaustion. You might find that you can maintain this level of masking for short periods but need extensive recovery time afterward.

Learning to be selective about when and where you mask can help preserve your energy for situations where it's most necessary. This might mean being more authentic in low-stakes social situations while saving your masking energy for important professional or social contexts.

Recovery strategies for introverted ADHD people need to address both social energy depletion and sensory overwhelm. Simple rest might not be sufficient if your nervous system is still processing stimulation from earlier experiences.

> ✗ **Danger Zone:** Avoid churches that equate extroverted participation with spiritual maturity or commitment. Quiet service can be just as valuable as visible involvement, and depth of faith isn't measured by social energy expenditure.

Effective recovery might involve complete sensory withdrawal: quiet environments, minimal visual stimulation, and reduced decision-making demands. You might need to avoid screens, conversations, and even background music during recovery periods. Some people find that activities like reading, gentle movement, or creative pursuits help them process and discharge overstimulation.

The timing of recovery is also important. Waiting until you're completely depleted often means needing longer recovery periods and experiencing more intense overwhelm. Building regular recovery time into your schedule can prevent complete depletion and help you function more sustainably.

Workplace challenges for introverted ADHD people often involve managing stimulation levels while maintaining productivity and professional relationships. Open office environments, frequent meetings, and collaborative work styles can be draining.

You might need to advocate for quieter work spaces, flexible scheduling that allows for recovery time, or modified communication styles that reduce the social energy required for professional interaction. Some people find that working from home or having access to private spaces helps them manage their stimulation levels more effectively.

The key is finding ways to meet your job requirements while honoring your temperamental and neurological needs. This might involve batching social interactions, taking strategic breaks, or finding roles that naturally accommodate introverted work styles.

Relationships with family and friends require clear communication about your needs for solitude and recovery time. People who care about you might interpret your need for alone time as rejection or lack of interest in the relationship.

Helping others understand that your need for solitude isn't about them but about how your brain and temperament process stimulation can prevent misunderstandings and hurt feelings. You can maintain close relationships while still honoring your need for recovery time.

Your support network might involve finding other introverted people who understand your energy limitations, connecting with online communities that don't require face-to-face interaction, or developing relationships that can be maintained through lower-energy communication methods.

Spiritual practices for introverted ADHD people might naturally gravitate toward contemplative traditions that emphasize silence, solitude, and internal processing. You might find that you connect with God more easily through quiet reflection than through group worship or social ministry.

This doesn't make you less spiritual or less committed to your faith. Different temperaments naturally connect with different spiritual practices, and God meets us where we are instead of requiring us to conform to extroverted spiritual expressions.

You might find meaning in practices like centering prayer, contemplative reading, nature-based spirituality, or other approaches that honor your need for quiet processing while engaging your ADHD brain's need for meaningful stimulation.

The goal isn't to become more extroverted or to push your limits constantly. The goal is to understand how your introversion and ADHD interact and to develop strategies that allow you to function sustainably while still engaging meaningfully with your work, relationships, and spiritual community.

Your introverted ADHD brain brings unique gifts to the world: deep thinking, careful observation, genuine empathy, and the ability to notice details that others miss. These gifts are best accessed when you honor your temperamental needs for quiet processing and recovery time.

Learning to advocate for your needs, set appropriate boundaries, and create environments that work for your combination of introversion and ADHD isn't selfishness—it's stewardship of the unique way God designed you to function and contribute to His kingdom.

Medication, Treatment, and Faith

"Is anyone among you sick? Let them call the elders of the church to pray over them and anoint them with oil in the name of the Lord. And the prayer offered in faith will make the sick person well; the Lord will raise them up." (James 5:14-15, NIV)

"Jesus went through all the towns and villages, teaching in their synagogues, proclaiming the good news of the kingdom and healing every disease and sickness." (Matthew 9:35, NIV)

"She said to herself, 'If I only touch his cloak, I will be healed.' Jesus turned and saw her. 'Take heart, daughter,' he said, 'your faith has healed you.' And the woman was healed at that moment." (Matthew 9:21-22, NIV)

You're standing in the pharmacy, holding a bottle of stimulant medication that your doctor prescribed for your ADHD, wrestling with questions that feel like they cut to the core of your faith. The rational part of your brain knows that ADHD is a neurological condition that can benefit from medical treatment. But the voice in your head, shaped by years of well-meaning but misguided spiritual advice, is whispering doubts: "Shouldn't prayer be enough? If God wanted to heal you, wouldn't He? Does taking this medication mean you don't have enough faith?"

Behind you in line, a woman is picking up insulin for her diabetes. Nobody would suggest that she's lacking faith for taking medication to manage a medical condition. But somehow, when it comes to brain-based conditions like ADHD, the waters get muddied with spiritual concerns about pharmaceutical dependence, the authenticity of mental health diagnoses, and whether seeking medical treatment demonstrates insufficient trust in God's power to heal.

You've heard the testimonies from the pulpit about miraculous healings and divine interventions. You've been prayed over by well-meaning church members who assured you that with enough faith, your ADHD symptoms would disappear. You've tried fasting, increased prayer time, spiritual warfare, and positive confession, hoping that the right combination of spiritual disciplines would fix your brain chemistry.

Some nights, when the medication is wearing off and your symptoms feel overwhelming, you wonder if you're somehow failing God by needing chemical assistance to function normally. Other days, when the medication helps you focus on your work, connect meaningfully with your family, and engage with your spiritual community without constant distraction, you feel grateful for the medical knowledge that made treatment possible.

> ★ **Pro Tip:** Track how medication affects your spiritual practices to optimize timing and dosage with your doctor. Note whether prayer feels easier at certain times of day, if focus during Bible study improves with medication, or if emotional regulation enhances worship experiences.

The tension between faith and medical treatment isn't new, but it gets more complicated with brain-based conditions because they affect behavior and personality — which makes them feel spiritual in a way that a broken leg doesn't. But the brain is an organ. ADHD is what happens when that organ's chemistry runs differently. Treating it isn't a failure of faith. It's stewardship.

God heals through whatever He chooses. Sometimes that's miraculous intervention. Sometimes it's the knowledge He built into medicine and the people who practice it. The Bible doesn't set these up as competing options — Luke was a physician, and Paul told Timothy to take wine for his stomach. The category of 'using medicine means you don't trust God' isn't a biblical one.

James 5:14-15 instructs believers to pray for the sick and promises that "the prayer offered in faith will make the sick person well." This doesn't mean that faith-based prayer is the only legitimate approach to illness, or that seeking medical treatment demonstrates a lack of faith. Throughout Scripture, we see examples of both miraculous healing and practical medical care being used by God to restore health.

Luke, who wrote both the Gospel of Luke and the book of Acts, was a physician. Paul, despite being used by God to perform miraculous healings, recommended wine to Timothy for his stomach problems instead of simply praying for healing. The Bible presents both spiritual and medical approaches to health as legitimate tools that God can use according to His wisdom and purposes.

Your ADHD brain is part of how God created you, but that doesn't mean that all aspects of your neurological differences are necessarily optimal for your wellbeing or effectiveness. Just as someone might need glasses to correct vision problems while still being "fearfully and wonderfully made," you might need medication to help your brain function more effectively while still being created intentionally by God.

The question isn't whether God could heal your ADHD miraculously—He certainly could. The question is whether He's chosen to provide healing through medical means, and whether you're open to receiving that healing in the form He's chosen to provide it. Refusing medication because you're waiting for miraculous healing might be like refusing to use the boat that God sent when you prayed for rescue from a flood.

★ **Pro Tip:** Prepare responses for people who question your medication use from a faith perspective. "God gave doctors wisdom to develop treatments that help His people function better" or "I take medication the same way someone with diabetes takes insulin" can shut down unhelpful spiritual advice.

Some Christians worry that taking ADHD medication means they're not trusting God to provide what they need. But this logic could be applied to any medical treatment, from antibiotics for infections to surgery for injuries. The same God who created your brain also gave humans the intelligence to develop medications that can help it function better.

Paul's instruction to Timothy to use wine for his stomach problems suggests that the apostles didn't view medical remedies as incompatible with faith. They understood that God often works through natural means to address physical problems, and that using available treatments can be part of good stewardship of the bodies He's given us.

Some believers worry that medication will somehow interfere with their spiritual growth or connection with God. But many people find that effective ADHD treatment enhances their spiritual life by reducing the distractibility, emotional dysregulation, and executive function challenges that can interfere with prayer, Bible study, and spiritual reflection.

> **⚠ Caution:** Avoid stopping medication during spiritual highs or seasons of strong faith without medical supervision. Your brain chemistry doesn't change based on your spiritual state, and medication supports your ability to engage with spiritual practices consistently.

When your brain is constantly scattered, overwhelmed, or dysregulated, it's difficult to engage deeply with spiritual practices or to sense God's presence and guidance. Medication that helps stabilize your attention and emotional state can create the mental space necessary for meaningful spiritual engagement.

> **✘ Danger Zone:** Avoid churches that teach medication use is incompatible with faith or demonstrates weak belief. God gave humans the ability to develop medical treatments for His people's benefit, and using available treatments can be an act of stewardship, not faithlessness.

Side effects require wisdom, patience, and good communication with your prescribing physician. You need to distinguish between temporary adjustment effects and genuine problems that need to be addressed. Some side effects are manageable with lifestyle adjustments, while others might require changing medications.

Prayer and spiritual discernment can play important roles in medication decisions, not by replacing medical advice but by helping you process the emotional and spiritual aspects of treatment. You can pray for wisdom in making treatment decisions, for minimal side effects, and for the medication to be effective in improving your symptoms.

The most effective treatment approaches for ADHD typically combine medication with behavioral strategies, lifestyle modifications, and environmental accommodations. Medication provides the neurochemical foundation that makes other interventions more effective, but it's not a complete solution by itself.

Therapy can help you develop coping strategies, address emotional challenges related to ADHD, and work through any spiritual or psychological barriers to effective treatment. ADHD coaching focuses on practical strategies for managing daily life challenges, while traditional therapy might address deeper emotional and relational issues.

The decision about medication is yours, your doctor's, and God's — in that order of practical involvement. It should be based on how significantly your symptoms affect your functioning, your relationships, and your ability to do what you believe you're called to do. It doesn't need to be permanent. You can try it, assess honestly, and adjust.

This decision doesn't need to be permanent. You can try medication for a period of time to see how it affects your symptoms and quality of life, then work with your doctor to adjust or discontinue treatment if needed. Many adults with ADHD use medication during demanding periods of their lives and then reduce or eliminate it when circumstances change.

Spiritual community can play important roles in supporting your treatment decisions, but this support needs to be based on accurate information about ADHD and medical treatment instead of spiritual misconceptions or stigma about mental health conditions.

> ★ **Pro Tip:** Find healthcare providers who understand both ADHD and faith concerns. You shouldn't have to choose between medical care and spiritual support, and providers who respect both aspects of your life provide better integrated treatment.

God's desire for your healing and wholeness isn't limited to spiritual restoration. He cares about your physical, emotional, and neurological wellbeing as well. Seeking effective treatment for ADHD can be part of stewarding the life and abilities He's given you instead of an indication of spiritual failure.

The woman with the bleeding disorder in Matthew 9 had spent years seeking medical treatment before encountering Jesus. Her previous medical attempts weren't seen as lack of faith but as reasonable efforts to address a serious health condition. When Jesus healed her, He commended her faith instead of criticizing her for having sought medical care.

Your faith can be expressed through gratitude for effective treatments, wisdom in making healthcare decisions, and trust that God can work through medical means to improve your quality of life. Taking medication doesn't mean you've given up on divine healing—it means you're open to receiving healing in whatever form God chooses to provide it.

The goal of ADHD treatment isn't just symptom management but helping you live the full, purposeful life that God intends for you. Whether that healing comes through medication, therapy, lifestyle changes, divine intervention, or some combination of approaches, the important thing is being open to the means God chooses to use in your situation.

Your ADHD brain is fearfully and wonderfully made, and seeking effective treatment is part of caring for the gift of life that God has given you. Don't let spiritual misconceptions prevent you from accessing treatments that could help you function more effectively and engage more fully with the purposes God has for your life.

> ⚠ **Caution:** Don't make medication decisions based on spiritual guilt or pressure from others. These are medical decisions that should involve qualified professionals who understand your brain chemistry and life circumstances.

The same God who created your unique brain also provided the knowledge and resources necessary to help it function optimally. Embracing both spiritual and medical approaches to ADHD isn't a sign of weak faith—it's a sign of wisdom and stewardship of the life He's entrusted to your care.

A Note for Pastors and Church Leaders

"He will not crush the weakest reed or put out a flickering candle." (Matthew 12:20, NIV)

"Carry each other's burdens, and in this way you will fulfill the law of Christ." (Galatians 6:2, NIV)

If someone handed you this book, they trust you. That matters more than whatever they underlined.

This chapter is written directly to pastors and church leaders, with the assumption that you entered ministry because you care about people — genuinely, specifically, individually. That assumption is being made in good faith. Everything that follows is offered in the same spirit.

You may have some resistance to the framing in this book. The language of neuroscience, ADHD diagnoses, and psychological frameworks can feel like it's importing a secular model into sacred space. That's a legitimate concern worth naming directly. But consider this: the God who knit each person together in their mother's womb (Psalm 139:13) knit their neurological wiring too. Caring about how a person's brain works isn't a concession to psychology. It's an extension of the pastoral care you're already called to provide.

Moses had a speech impediment. Elijah collapsed under a tree and asked to die. David wrote songs that swing from despair to exultation within a few verses. Peter acted before he thought, almost every time. Paul described a thorn in his flesh so persistent that he pleaded three times for God to remove it. The biblical narrative is full of people whose minds and nervous systems worked in ways that created real friction with the world around them. Neurodivergent believers aren't a modern category requiring a modern response. They're as old as the church itself.

What's new is that we now have language and research that helps us understand what's actually happening neurologically — why some people can't sit still, why criticism lands like a physical blow, why someone who genuinely loves God can't maintain a consistent quiet time no matter how hard they try. That understanding doesn't replace spiritual care. It makes spiritual care more accurate.

With that foundation, here are three things that would make your church more genuinely accessible to the neurodivergent people already sitting in your pews.

The first is awareness. Some percentage of your congregation has ADHD, autism, or both. The estimates run between 10 and 20 percent of the population, which means in a church of 100 people, somewhere between 10 and 20 of them are navigating a neurological difference that affects how they process information, regulate emotion, manage time, and experience social environments. Most of them have never told you. Most of them have spent years trying to pass as neurotypical in every environment including church, and they're exhausted by it.

You don't need a clinical background to develop this awareness. You need to know that when someone seems distracted during a sermon, they may not be disengaged — their brain may be processing what you're saying through movement or internal activity that looks like inattention but isn't. When someone leaves abruptly after a service, it may not be indifference — they may be overwhelmed and running on empty. When someone who seemed enthusiastic about a ministry role quietly disappears, it may not be flakiness — the structure of the commitment may have been incompatible with how their brain manages ongoing obligations.

None of this requires you to diagnose anyone. It requires you to hold your interpretations of people's behavior a little more loosely, and to stay curious about what's actually happening before you conclude you know.

The second thing is follow-through when people stop coming back. This is the one that matters most.

When someone disappears from your congregation — stops attending, stops responding, quietly drifts away — the easiest assumption is that life got busy or they found another church. Sometimes that's true. But for neurodivergent people, disappearance is often the end result of a specific experience that felt impossible to raise. A sermon that landed as personal condemnation. A ministry structure that was too much. An interaction that triggered a shame spiral they couldn't recover from. They didn't leave angry. They left depleted, and they didn't know how to explain why, and they assumed nobody would want to hear it anyway.

A single follow-up — not a form letter, a personal message or call — changes that equation significantly. Not to convince them to return. Not to fix whatever happened. Just to say: I noticed you were here and now you're not, and I wanted to check in. That's it. For someone whose entire history with institutions has involved being too much trouble to follow up with, that contact is not a small thing.

If you're not sure what to say, the words don't need to be elaborate. Something like: "Hey, I noticed we haven't seen you in a few weeks and wanted to check in — no agenda, just wanted to make sure you're okay." That's it. No ask attached, no assumption about why they left, no pressure to explain or return. Just acknowledgment that they existed in your congregation and you noticed they were gone. For someone who has spent years being invisible in institutional settings, that sentence is not nothing. It may be everything.

You won't be able to reach everyone. But the ones you do reach will remember it for years, because it will likely be the first time a church leader noticed they were gone.

The third thing is the hardest to say and the most important: see the people in front of you, not the metrics around them.

This isn't a criticism of church leadership — running a congregation requires attention to finances, attendance, programming, and growth. Those things are real and they matter. But neurodivergent people are unusually good at detecting when they're being processed as numbers rather than known as people. It's not paranoia. It's pattern recognition developed over a lifetime of being managed, categorized, and moved through systems that weren't designed for them.

When the sermon is primarily about giving, when the follow-up from the church is always tied to a financial ask, when the energy in the room is oriented toward growth metrics rather than the person sitting in the third row who hasn't smiled in three weeks — they notice. And they leave. Not with drama, usually. Just quietly, because the cost of staying got too high.

The antidote isn't complicated. It's the pastoral instinct you already have, applied more deliberately to the people who are easiest to miss — the ones who don't raise their hand, don't join the committee, don't put their name on anything, but show up every week and sit in the same seat and are hoping, maybe for the hundredth time, that this is the place where they finally fit.

Those people are in your church right now. Some of them are holding this book. They gave it to you because they don't know how to say these things out loud, and they're hoping you'll read it and recognize them.

You don't have to restructure your entire ministry to serve them well. You have to notice them. Reach out when they disappear. Preach to the person, not the pew.

That's the whole thing.

Conclusion: Embracing Your Neurodivergent Calling

"For I know the plans I have for you," declares the Lord, "plans to prosper you and not to harm you, to give you hope and a future." (Jeremiah 29:11, NIV)

"Before I formed you in the womb I knew you, before you were born I set you apart; I appointed you as a prophet to the nations." (Jeremiah 1:5, NIV)

"For we are God's handiwork, created in Christ Jesus to do good works, which God prepared in advance for us to do." (Ephesians 2:10, NIV)

The boy who couldn't sit still in church grew up to write a book about why that was never the problem.

That's not a redemption arc. It's a recognition — the moment when you realize that what everyone told you was wrong with you is what's most right about you. The ADHD traits that got you sent to the principal's office, that ended relationships, that made you feel like an outsider in every room including God's house — those traits have been doing something useful the whole time. You just didn't have the framework to see it.

You do now.

That doesn't mean it gets easy. Your brain will still misplace your keys, overcommit your calendar, and send the wrong email to the wrong person at the worst possible moment. You'll still have days where the gap between who you are and who you're trying to be feels impossible to close. Grace isn't a bypass around those days. It's what gets you through them.

What changes is what you do with the gap. Instead of treating every ADHD moment as evidence that you're fundamentally broken, you start treating it as information. Your brain needs something it isn't getting. The system you built isn't working. The environment is wrong for your wiring. These are solvable problems, not moral verdicts.

The church needs people who can't sit still. Not despite the restlessness — because of it. The most important work rarely gets done by people who are comfortable with how things are. It gets done by people whose brains won't let them look away from what needs fixing, who feel other people's pain at a volume that demands response, who make connections across ideas that more orderly thinkers would never put in the same room.

That's you.

Jeremiah 29:11 promises plans for hope and a future. Those plans were made knowing exactly how your brain is wired. They didn't account for a neurotypical version of you that doesn't exist. They were made for the actual you — scattered attention, emotional intensity, pattern recognition, and all.

Go do the work only you can do. Your ADHD brain isn't a liability you're managing around. It's the thing.

A Guide for Groups and Leaders

How to Use This Guide

This guide is designed for pastoral leadership teams, small groups, church staff, and anyone reading this book alongside others. It's organized around the book's six parts rather than individual chapters, so a group can cover the material in six sessions without requiring everyone to read at the same pace.

The questions are designed to generate conversation, not confirm comprehension. There are no correct answers. The goal is to create space for people to name their own experience — which, for neurodivergent people in particular, is often the thing that hasn't happened yet.

A few guidelines for facilitators:

Don't rush the silence. ADHD brains often need a moment before they can access what they actually think. Silence in a group discussion isn't failure — it's processing.

Don't require disclosure. Some questions invite personal sharing. Nobody should feel obligated to answer personally. The questions work as hypotheticals too.

Don't fix. If someone shares something difficult, the instinct to offer a solution or a scripture is understandable but often unhelpful. Acknowledgment first. Always.

The last section of questions is specifically for pastoral staff and church leaders. If you're using this guide in a mixed group, you can use those questions with everyone — they generate useful conversation regardless of role.

Part I: Foundation — Your Neurodivergent Identity in Christ

The book opens with the claim that ADHD traits are features, not flaws — part of how God intentionally designed certain minds. Does that framing resonate with you, or does it feel like a stretch? What would it take to believe it fully?

Have you ever been told — explicitly or implicitly — that your struggles with attention, consistency, or emotional regulation were spiritual failures? What did that cost you?

The author describes spending decades believing he was lazy, undisciplined, and spiritually immature before understanding his brain worked differently. How does a late diagnosis or late understanding of neurodivergence change the way you interpret your own history?

Paul's thorn in the flesh is presented as a parallel to ADHD — something God didn't remove but worked through. Is that comforting, frustrating, or both? Why?

Part II: Navigating Daily Life

The RSD chapter describes sitting in a sermon about sin and feeling personally condemned, even when the pastor was addressing a room of two hundred people. Have you experienced that? What happened afterward?

Masking — performing neurotypical behavior to fit in — is described as exhausting and isolating. How much of your energy goes into that performance in church settings specifically? What would it cost you to stop?

The book argues that traditional spiritual disciplines were designed for neurotypical brains, and that failure to maintain them isn't a spiritual problem. How does that land? What spiritual practices have actually worked for you, even if they look unconventional?

The author waited a year to be baptized because the church's scheduling process was too high a bar for his ADHD brain, and he nearly didn't do it. Have you ever nearly walked away from something spiritually significant because the institutional friction was too high?

Part III: Workplace and Calling

The book describes ADHD brains as poorly matched to traditional church ministry structures — weekly meetings, long-term committees, open-ended commitments — but well suited to crisis response, creative problem-solving, and empathy. Does that match your experience of ministry or service?

The author describes watching a church change from a people-focused pastoral culture to a money-focused one, and leaving. How do you evaluate whether a church's culture is compatible with your needs? What are the dealbreakers?

Creativity and innovation are presented as core ADHD strengths. Has your church or workplace ever benefited from your ADHD brain doing what it does naturally? Did anyone notice, or did the result get credit while the process got criticism?

The pastor chapter asks leaders to see people instead of metrics. For those of you who have been on the receiving end of metrics-focused ministry — where you felt processed rather than known — what did that feel like, and what would have been different?

Part IV: Special Challenges

The shame cycle described in this section — struggling, feeling guilty, using guilt as evidence of failure, seeking relief in the behavior that caused the guilt — is presented as neurological, not moral. Does reframing it that way change anything practically? Or does knowing the mechanism not make it easier to break?

The book says that healing from accumulated shame requires more than a verse about grace — it requires acknowledging that some of what you were told about yourself was simply wrong. Is there something specific you were told that you now believe was wrong? Have you been able to name that out loud before?

Addiction and impulse control are discussed as predictable consequences of how ADHD brains seek dopamine, not as character failures. How does the church you've experienced handle addiction — as a moral failing, a medical issue, or something else? What effect did that have on people who needed help?

Part V: Thriving

The book describes ADHD Christians who find a genuine home in church — who hyperfocus on worship, who find the right ministry role and feel like themselves for the first time. Has that happened for you? If so, what made it possible? If not, what's been in the way?

The Celebrating Strengths chapter reframes ADHD traits as capabilities developed at cost. Which of your ADHD traits has been most expensive to carry — and most valuable once it transferred to the right context?

The Support Systems chapter ends with: 'The right support system doesn't fix your ADHD. It changes what your ADHD costs you.' Who in your life has changed what your ADHD costs you? What did they do specifically?

The Parenting chapter says the legacy worth leaving is 'the kid who grew up watching a parent take their own brain seriously, ask for help without shame, and keep showing up even when it was hard.' Whether or not you're a parent — who modeled that for you? Who needed you to model it for them?

Part VI: Special Considerations and Closing

The AuDHD chapter describes the exhaustion of managing two neurotypes with competing needs simultaneously. For those who identify as AuDHD — or who love or lead someone who does — what does support actually look like in practice? What well-intentioned things have actually made it harder?

The Medication chapter addresses the theological discomfort some Christians feel about treating a brain-based condition medically. Have you experienced pressure — from a church, a pastor, or a community — to manage your ADHD spiritually rather than medically? What happened?

The conclusion ends: 'Go do the work only you can do. Your ADHD brain isn't a liability you're managing around. It's the thing.' What is the work only you can do? Have you started it?

For Pastoral Staff and Church Leaders

The book asks pastors to be aware that 10 to 20 percent of their congregation is navigating a neurological difference that affects how they receive preaching, participate in community, and sustain commitment. Does that number surprise you? Who comes to mind?

The follow-up section asks leaders to reach out personally when someone disappears — not to convince them to return, just to acknowledge they were there. Think of someone who stopped coming in the last year. What stopped you from reaching out? What would make that easier?

The book distinguishes between preaching style and theology — arguing that a guilt-and-condemnation preaching style can be neurologically inaccessible to RSD brains regardless of doctrinal accuracy. How do you think about your own preaching style in terms of who it reaches and who it may be inadvertently excluding?

The pastor chapter closes: 'You have to notice them. Reach out when they disappear. Preach to the person, not the pew.' What is one concrete thing you could change in your practice this week based on that?

About the Author

Richard Lowe discovered his ADHD diagnosis as an adult after years of struggling to understand why conventional approaches to faith, work, and relationships never seemed to fit. Raised in the Church of Christ, he left organized religion at fourteen due to the disconnect between his neurodivergent experience and traditional church expectations. After decades of spiritual searching, he found his way back to faith at Countryside Christian Church in Clearwater, Florida, where he was baptized in December 2024.

Drawing from personal experience navigating ADHD in Christian contexts, Richard writes with both vulnerability and insight about the intersection of neurodivergence and faith. His work focuses on helping ADHD Christians understand their neurological differences as divine design features instead of spiritual failures. When not writing, he enjoys photography and continues building communities of creative people, a habit he's had since long before he understood why and continues his own process of learning to thrive with an ADHD brain in a neurotypical world.

Richard lives in Clearwater, Florida and is passionate about creating more inclusive faith communities where neurodivergent believers can serve authentically without having to mask their differences.

Books by Richard Lowe

See books by Richard Lowe at
https://masterofworlds.com

Get free publishing insights and industry updates at
https://thewritingking.substack.com

For ghostwriting and book coaching services see
https://thewritingking.com